THE TEAM

Also by Kim Allan Johnson

The Gift

The Morning

El Regalo

THE TEAM

God's vision for His church is greater than you ever thought possible

Kim Allan Johnson

Pacific Press® Publishing Association
Nampa, Idaho
Oshawa, Ontario, Canada
www.pacificpress.com

Book design by Mark Bond for BONDesign, Inc.
Cover design resources from Erik Stenbakken

Library of Congress Cataloging-in-Publication Data

Johnson, Kim Allan, 1947–
The team : God's vision for his church is greater than you ever thought possible / Kim Allan Johnson.
p. cm.
ISBN-13: 978-0-8163-2203-9
ISBN-10: 0-8163-2203-1
1. Church. 2. Seventh-day Adventists—Doctrines. 3. trinity. I. Title.
BX6154. J62 2007
262'. 06732—dc22
2007060025

Additional copies of this book are available by calling toll-free 1-800-765-6955 or by visiting http://www.adventistbookcenter.com.

07 08 09 10 11 • 5 4 3 2 1

Dedication

Dedicated to my mother, Dorothy, whose carefully penned letters captured life so vividly.

Contents

Introduction

Early Sabbath morning, I peered out our kitchen window at the raging snowstorm that blanketed central Massachusetts. Suddenly the phone rang. "Hey, Kim," the head elder commented resignedly, "looks like we'll have to cancel church today."

I took the opportunity to expand his thinking and replied gently, "Actually, it's not possible to cancel church. We may not meet in the building with the pews in it at 337 Main Street, but we can't cancel because church is not a building or a worship service. It's people." Biblically speaking, we don't *go to* church, we *are* church every day.

The word *church* has suffered from similar distortions and misunderstandings for centuries. As a result, congregations struggle and members do not receive the help and encouragement they so desperately need.

The Scriptures use many different analogies to describe church, including army, temple, flock, living stones, body, and family. Each increases our understanding and helps fill in the mental picture. If the Bible was written today, it would most likely add to that list the word *team*.

A Christian editor recently commented, "When we do church as a team, we fulfill the Lord's desire that His Church work together—and we achieve amazing results for His kingdom."[1]

Connecting church with the word *team* resonates because it is a word people can relate to from their life experience. There are not only athletic teams but also teams of doctors, engineers, climbers, researchers, rescuers, builders, and others.

The word *team* conveys almost universal images of togetherness, mutual support, and the blending of talents and abilities to become something together that is much greater than any of us could be alone. Jesus modeled team building in a stunning way by taking a motley, self-centered band of twelve men and shaping them into a force that literally changed the world. He took the concept of *team* to extraordinary heights and defined it in jaw-dropping ways.

We are now called to continue His work and live out His thrilling dream in our own day, a dream that the Godhead has had for the church since the days of Old Testament Israel. Scripture makes it abundantly clear that our success as individual Christians depends on our understanding and experiencing church as God intended it to be. The success of God's loving ministry in a world plagued by hopelessness and strife depends on our being church together according to His plan.

This book, ***The Team,*** will take you on a remarkable journey that explores God's special calling for the Seventh-day Adventist Church and reveals how that high calling can revolutionize each of our lives today.

Kim Allan Johnson

---

1 Cited in http://www.amazon.com/Doing-Church-Team-Wayne-Cordeiro/dp/0830736808, March 5, 2007.

Chapter 1

Phase Three

It seemed like a clever idea at the time. My wife Ann was "great with child," our first. In mere days we would be parents! I knew that shortly after the contractions started she would phone her doctor to see if it was time to hightail it to the hospital. I thought, *Hey, why not capture that special moment for posterity?* Without telling her, I placed a tape recorder on the desk near the phone, inserted a fresh tape, and waited.

Sure enough, late one Friday afternoon the contractions began. They came sporadically at first and then grew in intensity and frequency. I faithfully wrote each one down in a little blue spiral-bound notebook, just as I had been taught in birthing class. Finally, I heard Ann say the magic words, "I've got to call the doctor."

As she waddled slowly and awkwardly toward the den, I followed close behind, sporting a huge smirk. I was about to capture one of those motherly moments you read about in *Ladies' Home Journal* or *Woman's Day* magazines. As Ann dialed, I quietly stepped up to the other end of the desk, extended a nervous index finger, and hit "record."

If I played back the recording today, you'd hear my wife saying something like, "What on earth are you doing over there? Are you recording this? This is no time to be fooling around with that ridiculous thing." So much for motherly moments. She was a little tense, but she was also right. There were much more important matters to attend to.

Within an hour and a half, I was sitting by her bedside in the maternity ward garbed in a faded blue expectant-daddy getup, including monk cap and booties. I had three major responsibilities: hold her hand, feed her ice chips, and warn of upcoming contractions by monitoring a machine with a green screen that was wired to her bulging belly.

As the night wore on, Ann scrunched my left hand in a numbing death grip. The nurse kept the ice bucket replenished. I watched the monitoring machine with the intensity of a dog eyeing a backyard barbecue. "Oh, oh, a contraction's coming," I told her nervously. I could see the thin blue line on the monitor rise up to a rounded peak and then slowly subside. The higher the peak, the worse the pain.

"O-o-o-o," I continued minutes later, "this one looks like a whopper. We're talking serious pain here! Get a grip on those bedrails, baby! You're in for a real teeth-grinder!" I was trying to be helpful.

After long hours of torment, my wife was finally wheeled into the delivery room.

And there, about 4:00 A.M., our little daughter was born. She weighed twenty-two pounds and was nine inches long. (Or was it nine pounds and twenty-two inches? I can never keep that straight.)

Today the Seventh-day Adventist Church is also experiencing a birth of sorts. Our ecclesiastical ankles are swollen. Our denominational back is aching. New life is coming. We are on the front edge of a new thing that the Holy Spirit is earnestly attempting to do in our midst. I call this new life "Phase 3."

Phase 1

Since joining the church in 1968, I have experienced three separate and distinct phases of Adventism. I had no Adventist upbringing and became a church member during Phase 1 after transferring from engineering school to a little Adventist college in rural New England. I chose to major in theology. Those were the waning days of legalism, when we heard a lot about prophecy and doctrine but very little about Jesus. I will be eternally grateful for the Bible studies people gave me that resulted in my baptism, but I now realize that they were long on beasts and short on the Savior. I knew numbers and timelines and heads and horns and metals and nightmarish end-time scenarios. But the picture was incomplete. I fell in love with truth rather than with Christ, who is the Truth.

Legalism produces bucketloads of guilt, which can be a powerful motivator, and back then I felt guilty about pretty much everything in my life. I tried very hard to make myself acceptable to God. All during Phase 1 I poured myself into things religious with that uniquely frenetic energy characteristic of those who depend on their works to be saved.

I majored in extracurricular activities in college, trying every way I knew to spread truth. I became part of a mediocre folk group that traveled all over New England singing and preaching. I was the bulky-haired, guitar-strumming, intense-looking guy in the back. I cringe now when I think of all the guilt my sermons inadvertently dumped on the faithful.

I was eventually appointed the official outreach coordinator for the whole college, which provided untold opportunities for proving my spiritual worthiness to God. Within weeks I launched a massive plan to share Bible truth with all of Boston and any other nearby city that might be interested.

In order to raise much-needed cash for the cause, I stumbled into a fund-raising fiasco. An overzealous salesman phoned me one day in the dorm and described an incredibly simple way to fill our bare coffers. All I had to do was get fifty students to sell an eclectic variety of doodads and baubles door to door in the community. After overhead, we could keep 50 percent! The numbers were truly impressive. Just one case of the stuff could net us twenty-five dollars. With visions of big bucks for the witnessing budget, I must have ordered at least a hundred cases. Confident of off-the-charts success, I promised that the person who sold the most would get a brand-new, one-hundred-dollar, easy-touch Royal typewriter.

We off-loaded the goods from the delivery van and stored them in an unused building on campus. On the big day only a dozen students showed up. Undaunted, I gave a rousing speech about lost people, hell, and the glories of the Promised Land. The students fanned out all over town toting multicolored feather dusters, multicolored key rings attached to what looked like oversized plastic marbles, multicolored notepads, multicolored pencils, etc.

At the end of the campaign we had ninety-seven cases left, and I was in big trouble. I pleaded with the company like a druggie before a judge, and they graciously let me truck the leftovers back to headquarters without penalty.

During the ensuing months, I slipped more fully into the insecure spiritual role of those who are high on commitment but short on spiritual assurance and inner peace. At some point I found an inch-thick, yellow-jacketed book ominously entitled *Sin.* I read it with the earnestness of a pathologist studying life-sapping diseases. The book opened up vast new possibilities for self-righteousness to flourish and expand. By the time I turned the last page, avoiding sin had become a near obsession. (My roommate would probably have left off the word *near.*)

I started dressing in the most subdued colors I could find from my limited wardrobe. Who knew if a particular color might be too flashy or ostentatious? The book had a whole chapter on that particular type of violation. I was fully prepared to wear black socks, black shoes, black pants, black shirts, and black underwear every day, if that's what it took to be holy.

The union conference decided to send a bunch of us students to Bermuda to revive the youth. It was more of a vacation than a mission. We met briefly in the morning for a devotional and then hopped on our mopeds to tour the island. In the evening we simply had to show up at a rally.

Sadly, on the flight home, the other students got into a prolonged, rather shocking period of silliness. They laughed uproariously at every little thing. It was the kind of laughter you experience around 2:00 A.M. when you're pulling an all-nighter before a big exam. It was like a mass case of the hiccups. They guffawed for hours.

As I sat in my window seat staring out at the puffy cumulous-cloud formations, I recalled another helpful section of the book on sin that zeroed in on that kind of abject frivolity. My heart filled with utter disdain. *Look at them,* I thought. *And they call themselves Christians?* By the time I arrived back at the dorm, I had determined to never laugh again. Who knew at what juncture it might spill over into evil? Why take the chance with so much at stake? To paraphrase a famous quote, constant vigilance was the price of holiness. Spiritual life became an onerous burden.

Phase 2

Eventually I was delivered from legalism by discovering the wonders of grace and righteousness by faith during Phase 2. Around 1970 revival leaped from campus to campus across the U.S. As part of that resurgence, someone gave me a copy of the remarkable little book *Steps to Christ* that taught me, for the first time, how to trust in Christ completely for forgiveness, acceptance, and spiritual growth. I read mind-boggling sentences such as, "You cannot atone for your past sins; you cannot change your heart and make yourself holy. But God promises to do all this for you through Christ. . . . If you believe the promise,—believe that you are forgiven and cleansed,—God supplies the fact; you are made whole."[1]

The author went on to say, "Through this simple act of believing God, the Holy Spirit has begotten a new life in your heart. You are as a child born into the family of God, and He loves you as He loves His Son."[2]

The thrill of hearing those words is at the top of my life experiences. I was so excited that I even contemplated buying a plaid suit. The words of Scripture jumped off the pages with new meaning: "for all have sinned and fall short of the glory of God, being justified freely by His grace through the redemption that is in Christ Jesus" (Romans 3:23, 24,

NKJV). And "For by grace you have been saved through faith, and that not of yourselves; it is the gift of God, not of works, lest anyone should boast" (Ephesians 2:8, 9, NKJV).

Several other theology majors and I kept a small version of *Steps to Christ* in our back pockets and read to other students from its grace-filled pages. Some English majors labeled us "resident holies," but we were undeterred. We gave them over to the devil and kept on quoting.

Those were heady times. Soon I was caught up once again in grand schemes to reach the lost. But this time I was experiencing righteousness by faith in my own heart. I had a Christ-centered message of hope and tapped into a far more healthy motivation.

Unfortunately, the transition from Phase 1 to Phase 2 was not without considerable denominational pain, misunderstanding, and finger-pointing throughout North America. For a time, Adventists across the country were polarized. Each side hurled charges and countercharges. Leaders called special councils and committee meetings to sort out entrenched conflict. The Holy Spirit had to work overtime to move churches forward into grace, inch by precious inch.

But thirty years later, grace-oriented sermons have now become the norm, and books about righteousness by faith fill the shelves of every Adventist Book Center. Except among some battle-hardened holdouts, Phase 2 has been widely accepted.

Phase 3

We are now on the brink of what I believe is Phase 3. In Phase 2 we learned how to have a successful Christian experience *individually*. In Phase 3 the Holy Spirit is earnestly trying to teach us how to be successful Christians *together*. Phase 3 is all about discovering how to be church.

It is certainly an incredible miracle for individuals to turn from sin and give their hearts to Christ. But it is an equally incredible miracle for them to join hearts and minds to become the body of Christ. Taking church members from disparate backgrounds and cultures, with a wide variety of personalities, hang-ups, and biases, and bringing them together into true unity, interdependence, and mutual love, is the relentless focus of the Godhead in our day. They are now engaged in prodding, urging, and wooing us all into being church in new and unprecedented ways.

So many of our churches in North America are languishing and struggling with stagnant growth and little vitality, and I have often wondered why. I now believe that in many cases it is because they have no clue how to be church in the biblical sense. We put a bunch of baptized people in a building with pews and a pulpit and tell them to be a church without explaining how. Is it any wonder they flounder so?

In my seminar called "Church Alive," about God's vision for the church, we take part in a group exercise I call the blind circle. I ask volunteers to come forward, stand in a circle, and join hands. (They have to be in multiples of four, such as eight or twelve). I tell each group that they can talk but they have to close their eyes and keep them shut on penalty of death. I explain that the object is to form a square. It is hilarious to watch as they try to agree on how it should be done. When they feel they have made a decent square, I have them open their eyes. Usually, through trial and error, they do remarkably well.

I then ask what they think was the key to success. The most frequent answers are cooperation, listening, and leadership. As important as those are, there is a factor that is more fundamental and more important than any of those. The vital key is that everyone understood what I meant when I said "square." Everyone could picture that clearly in their minds because they had been taught since childhood exactly what a square looked like—four straight lines the same length put together at ninety-degree angles. *The point is that you cannot make what you do not know.* If I had asked them to make a Deedilyfump, they couldn't do it. They'd flounder all night and be no closer to the solution than when they started because no one knows what a Deedilyfump is, not even me. Likewise, we cannot expect our members to "be church" when they have so many different ideas of what church is all about.

How we do church is usually based on what previous generations have done or the pooling of our own subjective opinions. Most planning assumes that we know the answer to the crucial question, "What is church?" Sadly we press ahead with budgets and committee meetings and programming and all sorts of activities without ever seriously addressing that vital question.

Stephen Covey, in his best-selling book, *The Seven Habits of Highly Effective People,* tells the story of an imaginary group of people on safari cutting their way through the jungle with machetes. They hack and sweat and slog along day after day through thick underbrush and vines.

One day someone decides to climb up the tallest tree in the area. The person looks around and yells down, "Wrong jungle!"

Covey concludes, "As individuals, groups, and businesses, we're often so busy cutting through the undergrowth we don't even realize we're in the wrong jungle. . . . Effectiveness ... does not depend solely on how much effort we expend, but on whether or not the effort we expend is in the right jungle."[3] So, what jungle has your church been hacking around in lately?

Remarkably, even though we think of ourselves as "people of the Bible," several key doctrines in Scripture often are either ignored or followed to a very limited degree: (1) the priesthood of all believers; (2) the biblical role of the pastor; (3) becoming the body of Christ; (4) spiritual gifts; (5) building a sense of community among the members; and (6) incarnational evangelism, among other examples. These truths are just as important as the Sabbath and the Second Coming. Whenever they are not valued, the congregations suffer. All of these biblical teachings come under the heading of "ecclesiology," the biblical doctrine of how to be church.

Do your congregation and local leadership make understanding the Godhead's vision for the church top priority? Does the Trinity's grand expansive plan grip their hearts and imaginations so powerfully that sometimes they can't sleep at night? When the church leaders meet, do they spend most of their time strategizing how Heaven's plan can become a reality in their congregation and community?

Or does the church board spend their time discussing whether to buy a new lawnmower, whether to raise the janitor's salary by fifty cents an hour, or what color to paint the Junior room? Are the leaders' priorities in line with God's, or are they majoring in minors? What story does the agenda tell?

"Processionary caterpillars" are very interesting little critters. They move through the trees in long processions, each one with its eyes half closed and its head snugly fitted up against the rear of its predecessor.

> Jean-Henri Fabre, the great French naturalist, after patiently experimenting with a group of these caterpillars, finally enticed them to the rim of a large flowerpot where he succeeded in getting the first one connected with the last one, thus forming a complete circle that started moving around in a procession that had neither a beginning nor an end.
>
> The naturalist expected that after a while the caterpillars would catch on to the joke—get tired of their useless march and start off in some new direction.
>
> But not so.
>
> Through sheer force of habit, the living, creeping circle kept moving around the rim of the pot—around and around, keeping the same relentless pace for seven days and seven nights—and doubtless would have continued longer had it not been for sheer exhaustion and ultimate starvation.
>
> An ample supply of food was close at hand, and plainly visible, but it was outside the range of the circle so the caterpillars continued along the beaten path. They were following instinct, habit, custom, tradition, precedent, past experience, standard practice, or whatever you may choose to call it, but they were following blindly.
>
> ... **They meant well—but they got nowhere.**[4]

In a similar manner, Adventist congregations today may blindly follow the past, assuming that the way we have done church up until now is the way it is supposed to be. As a result, they find themselves on a treadmill of tradition that falls far short of what the Godhead originally had in mind.

A startling prophecy in the book of Revelation indicates that in the last days a people would arise who have excellent doctrines and lots of truth, and yet, they would attempt to be church according to their own thinking. The results would be so off the mark, so disastrously out of whack, that it would make God nauseous. " 'And to the angel of the church of the Laodiceans write, " 'I know your works, that you are neither cold nor hot. . . . So then, because you are . . . neither cold nor hot, I will spew you out of My mouth' " ' " (Revelation 3:14–16, NKJV).

These verses are not targeting individual Christians. The focus is squarely on our approach to being church as congregations, not just Sabbath morning but every day of the week. The issue is not primarily worship or programming but relationships.

A church may be full of dedicated, sincere, active Christians and yet fit the Loadicean description because they are trying to be church according to their own plans, their own methods, and their own ideas and values. And God is saying, "Not even close." The mental image of God holding His hand over His mouth as He stifles the urge to barf is pretty graphic, to say the least. This is not a pleasant picture.

Yet, God is not reacting that way out of anger. He loves us so fully, so immensely, that His great heart is pained by either our neglect or our rejection of His plan. It is the reaction of a farmer who has provided people with enough land and seeds to feed thousands of starving children, and yet they fail to water or fertilize and are content with a relatively meager harvest. It is the reaction of an architect who provided people with all the blueprints and resources to build a magnificent structure for shade and protection from the cold, and yet they insist on erecting a tent. It is deep disappointment and sadness that forces God to reach for the Maalox.

I have to confess that it is extremely disconcerting to me, as a convert to Adventism, that we so readily agree that the Laodicean prophecy applies to the Adventist Church and yet seem to do so very little about it.

"Yup, that's us, all right. The way we do church makes God wanna puke." Yet in the thirty years I've been a member, I can't think of any major changes in the fundamental direction of the church in North America. Even though God is yelling down at us, "Wrong jungle!" we continue hacking and cutting in the same basic path.

However, the Holy Spirit is starting to change that alarming, frustrating scenario. He is moving upon hearts and minds throughout Adventism. He is working the same way He did to transition us from legalism to righteousness by faith. There will once again be misunderstandings and finger-pointing. Charges and countercharges will be flung at each other. Power struggles will erupt.

But new life is inexorably being born. It starts with a deep longing in the heart. I see it when I speak to various groups throughout the country. After I talk about God's vision for His church, pastors here and there will come up to me privately and say, "I am so anxious to see the vision you are talking about become a reality, but my conference is still stuck in the old paradigm. What can I do?" Someday, somehow, someway, through courageous, submissive cooperation with the Holy Spirit, that is going to change. I just hope I'm not in a nursing home by the time it does.

Each of us longs for significance. We live day after day, doing the best we can, hoping that our lives will, in the end, count for something good. We wonder if, in spite of our failures and weaknesses, we are making a difference in the lives of others. I know of no greater way to develop a sense of significance amidst our daily routine than to partner with the Godhead in the fulfillment of Their amazing vision for the church. There is no more exalted purpose, no higher privilege, than to know you have a part to play each day in the fulfillment of the Godhead's dream.

---

1 Ellen G. White, *Steps to Christ*, p. 51.

2 Ibid., p. 52.

3 Stephen Covey, *The Seven Habits of Highly Effective People* (New York: Simon and Schuster, 1989), p. 101.

4 Roger Fritz, *Think Like a Manager* (Shawnee Mission, Kans.: National Press Publications, 1991), p. 97.

Chapter 2

Inheritors of the Dream

About twelve years ago my wife and I plowed through a host of challenges to build our first home. The bank wanted five thousand dollars for a down payment. We emptied our savings account, cracked open our piggy bank, broke into our daughter's Snoopy bank, and fished under cushions for any coins among the fallen food scraps and dust, but we were still short.

"What now?" we puzzled. After I ranted and raved about the unfairness of not being born into a wealthy family, we settled on the time-tested, traditional American solution—hit up the relatives.

I grew up amidst stacks of overdue bills. The only "savings" Mom and Dad had were eight books of green stamps from the A&P supermarket. They were a dry hole.

My wife's parents proved to be a more lucrative source. They had paid cash for their house, which was definitely a good omen. They graciously loaned us the rest of the money we needed—about $4,926.00. They insisted that it be a gift, but I dutifully told them we'd repay every single cent, which was pretty much like a chimpanzee promising the zookeeper he'd pay back every banana.

We spent weeks designing our dream house on sketchpads. Just the right size living room, just the right kind of open architecture for the kitchen and dining area, and so on. Next we selected a highly recommended contractor from among three candidates. He turned out to be a very nice guy to work with—until we signed the contract. After that he became a pit bull with a toothache. We were yelled at, lectured to, and criticized, as if we were at fault for intruding on his precious time and having the audacity to ask him to follow our plan. He eventually sent out a crew that included a guy with several missing teeth and the vacant stare of someone for whom the word *high* had more than one meaning.

We moved in three or four months later, around mid-February. Within two weeks the roof leaked. That night I spent hours up there under the stars, in subzero weather, shoveling off knee-deep snow to stop the flow. Five weeks later the pump in our septic system went on strike. Three months after that we couldn't open the front door because the house had gotten tired of standing upright and sagged down onto it. That summer several pieces of siding had a hissy fit about having to protect our walls against bad weather and chose to fall off in protest. We got news from the local lab that there was too much lead in our water. The floor in the kitchen developed a creative camel hump smack-dab in the middle. You get the picture.

We were bitterly disappointed. Over the next several years we fixed everything, but I will never build a house from scratch again. Not even for free. It's way too much grief. I don't want to hear your happy testimonials. I know the truth. How different our experience could have been if the contractor had simply listened to our ideas and followed our plans.

Long ago, the Godhead dreamed about building something. They created the grandest, most compelling design in the entire universe. Every facet was to be infused with Their values and character. What made it wonderfully unique was that it wouldn't be built with wood and concrete but with *people.* They named it "church." The Trinity longs for us to faithfully follow Their design, to give Their plan top priority.

The story of why the church was brought into existence is thrilling in its scope and purpose. It is a story that takes us back before Creation itself.

The Father, Son, and Holy Spirit are the Center of the universe. They are the Source. They are the Heroes in the plan of salvation.

For unlimited millennia, however, They were all that was. The Godhead existed in empty space, in a sublime, all-pervasive vacuum. No angels, no unfallen worlds, no stars, no planets, no comets, no human beings, no animals, no trees, no orchids or monarch butterflies.

They were never lonely because no Member of the Godhead has ever been alone. They've always had each Other, which was always enough. They loved each Other with an infinite, unconditional love that was more powerful and intense than we can ever hope to fully comprehend.

One day, that love spilled over and became creation. Because the very essence of Their love is to give and to serve, They made everything for creation's sake, not Their own. Untold numbers of worlds were brought into existence, perhaps millions of years before ours, filled with beings and natural phenomena that would be completely foreign to our understanding today.

The thing that those beings throughout the cosmos marveled at the most was how intensely the Father, Son, and Holy Spirit loved them. That love was the favorite topic of discussion in every home, at every workplace, at every school, and on every outing.

The Trinity regularly spent large amounts of time with the inhabitants on every planet. They taught them, walked with them, praised and encouraged them, hugged them, guided them, explained the intricacies of nature to them, involved them in challenging projects and assignments, and always provided far more than they hoped for and honored their dreams.

The Godhead's energies were focused exclusively on bringing others joy and fulfillment. Throughout all creation, They were spontaneously worshiped and universally cherished.

At some point, tragically, sin entered the cosmos when Lucifer inexplicably chose to rebel, taking one-third of the angels with him. The

Trinity suddenly became the enemy. They endured slander, innuendo, gossip, and lies from the very ones They had loved so deeply for so long.

Finally, revolt escalated into open warfare. The Godhead knew that the only thing that could win back disaffected hearts was a deeper revelation of Their love. But that love had already been lavishly disclosed. Nothing had been held back. The fallen angels had worked closely with the Trinity and knew Their hearts extremely well. There was, therefore, no greater revelation of love the Godhead could employ to win back their loyalty and affection. The situation was utterly, heartbreakingly hopeless.[1]

The sickening tragedy took on even wider dimensions with the rebellion of Adam and Eve. The human race now became infected with sin and selfishness, which would be passed on from generation to generation.

But humanity's situation was different from that of the rebellious angels. Sinful man had not yet understood or experienced the fullness of divine love. There was still hope if human beings could see the astonishing value the Trinity placed on them and the astounding price They were willing to pay to win them back. Sinners needed to know how deeply They longed to embrace the most hardened rebels and heal the most obnoxious purveyors of evil.

In order to accomplish this vitally important task, the Trinity came up with a bold, audacious plan that must have stunned all of heaven. I can imagine residents of far-flung worlds giving each other incredulous looks, trying to comprehend it. After careful consideration, the Godhead decided to bring together a group of Their *enemies* on planet Earth to portray Them to the human race. This highly privileged group of sinners would make known the Trinity's values and priorities; would mirror Their relationships; and would express the power of Their unconditional love.

As the Father, Son, and Holy Spirit related the plan more fully, it became even more inexplicable. They explained that the earthly rebels would be utilized to seal the loyalty of unfallen beings and secure the cosmos from future ruin.

More than one heavenly being must have thought, *I don't get it. Wouldn't it be better if the Trinity sent a large contingent from one of our planets that has never sinned? They would have a much greater chance of representing the Godhead well. Why use these crude, self-centered, corrupt people from earth?*

Imagine the United Nations asking a couple of New York City gangs to represent them at peace talks in the Middle East. Picture Enron's former executives representing Mother Teresa at a conference on ministry to the poor. Neither of these scenarios makes sense. And it made even less sense for sinners to represent the Godhead. But that's exactly the path They chose. They would first get some of the earthly rebels to become loyal followers and infuse them with new life. This band would then grow and expand until it became the most powerful force in the world.

Portraying the character of the Trinity has always been the church's primary purpose. That is the only real justification for its existence. Anything less is a distortion. Anything less is simply a religious club.

My father was a weekend drunk. He and Mom had lots of yelling matches. I don't remember them holding each other's hand once. When I got married I didn't really have a clue what true love was all about or how to be a good partner. I was domineering, critical, and moody, not to mention my juvenile fascination with burping.

Not long after our lovey-dovey wedding ceremony there was trouble. On the second evening of our honeymoon, my wife and I attended a concert at the Kennedy Center in Washington, D.C., to hear the famous cellist, Mstislav Rostropovich. A thoughtful friend had given us tickets as a gift.

After the concert, I suddenly overreacted big-time to something innocuous that came up in our conversation. I lost it. And in order to make my wife fully aware of my displeasure, I chose to not talk to her for the next *two days*.

I cringe now when I think of what an idiot I was to treat her like that. Not good. But being controlling and withdrawing was the model I had been given during childhood. After counseling, a lot of forgiveness by my spouse, and extensive trial and error, I eventually learned a much better way. True love can be extremely difficult to understand if there is no example, no model to observe.

It is nearly impossible to understand the love of the Godhead without a concrete example, a living demonstration. The church was brought into existence specifically for that lofty purpose, to reveal the Trinity's love.

The very first church was formed in Old Testament times. God looked over the entire earth and found a large group of slaves in Egypt that could trace their lineage back to Abraham. These Israelites had been brutalized and oppressed for generations, with no advantages and no privileges. Life was a harrowing dance with death. At an overseer's whim, any family member could be murdered or locked away.

"Therefore they set taskmasters over them to afflict them with their burdens. And they built for Pharaoh supply cities, Pithom and Raamses. . . . So the Egyptians made the children of Israel serve with rigor. And they made their lives bitter with hard bondage—in mortar, in brick, and in all manner of service in the field. All their service in which they made them serve was with rigor" (Exodus 1:11–14, NKJV).

These exploited people were woefully deficient in education, refinement, and moral sensibility. They were ignorant, untrained, and degraded. Many of them had lost their knowledge of the true God and His law. They were confused by false teachings and corrupted by long interaction with the heathen.[2] They even joined the Egyptians in their worship of the sun, moon, stars, animals, and images.[3]

This was the starting point for God's grand vision! One of the key reasons the Lord selected them was because the lower the starting point, the greater the miracle. The more stunning the transformation, the more God would be elevated in the eyes of the heathen nations.

The prophet Isaiah states clearly that the church of Israel was raised up specifically to reveal God. He talks about God's glory, which is His character of love:[4]

- *"The glory of the* L*ORD shall be revealed,*
  And all flesh shall see it together;

For the mouth of the Lord has spoken" (Isaiah 40:5, 6, NKJV; italics supplied).

- "And he said unto me, Thou art my servant; Israel, *in whom I will be glorified*" (Isaiah 49:3, ASV; italics supplied).

- "Arise, Jerusalem! Let your light shine for all the nations to see! *For the glory of the Lord is shining upon you.* Darkness as black as night will cover all the nations of the earth, but the glory of the Lord will shine over you. All nations will come to your light. Mighty kings will come to see your radiance" (Isaiah 60:1–3, NLT; italics supplied).

The Israelites were called to fulfill an incredibly lofty plan. In the preamble to the Ten Commandments, God made it abundantly clear that any success would come from Him as the Source: " 'I am the Lord your God, who brought you out of the land of Egypt, out of the house of bondage' " (Exodus 20:2, NKJV).

In this introduction God is, in effect, saying to Israel, "I want to build you into a team of winners and champions of love, committed to excellence. But don't think for a second that you can get there on your own. You will be just as dependent on Me to free you from the bondage of sin and selfishness as you were to be freed from bondage in Egypt. How many plagues were you able to produce? How often have you parted the Red Sea? Now I will be the Source of another miracle—within you."

In order to reflect the complex, multifaceted nature of the Trinity, Israel was to be the recipient of extraordinary talents and abilities from God.

1. The Israelite nation was to become a nurturing community of faith[5] (see Leviticus 19:18, 34).
2. Israelites would be renowned for their love and service to others.[6] Hurting, rejected, powerless individuals from all over the globe

could find in Israel a warm, sympathetic reception. Strangers would be treated as family. Israelites were to be the Red Cross and Salvation Army of their day.[7] *"But the stranger that dwelleth with you shall be unto you as one born among you, and thou shalt love him as thyself; for ye were strangers in the land of Egypt"* (Leviticus 19:34, KJV; italics supplied).

3. Israel was to become a nation of *intellectual giants.*[8] The nation's leadership was supposed to be filled with people like Joseph and Daniel who would regularly be recognized in today's terms as *Time*'s Man of the Year. Israel's university scientists would make continuous breakthroughs and dominate the list of Nobel Prize winners of their day. "Behold, I have taught you statutes and judgments, . . . that ye should do so in the land whither ye go to possess it. *Keep therefore and do them; for this is your wisdom and your understanding in the sight of the nations, which shall hear all these statutes, and say, Surely this great nation is a wise and understanding people"* (Deuteronomy 4:5, 6, KJV; italics supplied).
4. Their *craftsmanship* would be the marvel of the world.[9] The label "Made in Israel" would be coveted everywhere. Their skill, creativity, and innovation were to be legendary.
5. Israel would be recognized far and wide as experts in agriculture and animal husbandry.[10] Crop failure would disappear.[11] The land was to be returned to the Edenic beauty Adam and Eve knew so well.[12]
6. Mental, emotional, and physical disease would be virtually unknown among them.[13] Their robust health and life expectancy would dwarf that of others.
7. They were not to be hermits or isolationists. The heathen would come to Israel and then return home to tell what they had seen (see Isaiah 55:5). But Israel was also to fulfill the gospel commission to "Go" by conquering new territory, expanding the influence of the gospel in ever widening circles. The gospel would also be spread by God scattering Israelites among the heathen.[14]

8. With God's blessing, these lowly slaves would far surpass Egypt and eventually become the greatest nation on earth, and their territory would span the globe.[15] *"If you fully obey the LORD your God and carefully follow all his commands I give you today, the LORD your God will set you high above all the nations on earth"* (Deuteronomy 28:1, NIV; italics supplied). Israel would be God's instrument to bring peace and joy to millions.[16] History books were to be filled with accounts, not of Egypt, Babylon, Persia, or Rome but of great Israel.

It was an incredible vision. From the lowest to the highest. All of these qualities and accomplishments were intended to reveal to the world *the life of the Trinity itself.* The relationships, values, and priorities that characterized Israel would portray to all peoples the principles of God's kingdom.[17] Within the nation's loving, nurturing community, sinners would become extraordinarily whole.

Tragically, Israel ultimately turned its back on Heaven's amazing plan.[18] The wayward, headstrong nation failed to live up to the Godhead's hopes and dreams and lost sight of Heaven's vision. As the Scriptures warn, "Where there is no vision, the people perish" (Proverbs 29:18, KJV).

On April 4, 1973, an elaborate ribbon-cutting ceremony marked the opening of the massive World Trade Center in New York City. It became known as a building project unlike any other. The complex consisted of twin towers, four low-rise structures, a five-acre plaza with shops and restaurants, and several levels for parking and storage. Each tower rose 110 stories into the sky. Constructed over seven years at a cost of over seven hundred million dollars, it offered ten million square feet of office space.

The architects for the project were Minoru Yamasaki, Phillip Roth and Sons. The lead engineers were John Skilling and Leslie Robertson of Worthington, Skilling, Helle, and Jackson. They spent years in planning, overcame hundreds of obstacles, attended to countless details, and ultimately created in Manhattan one of the most magnificent building complexes in the world.[19]

We all know what happened on September 11, 2001. Two commercial jets piloted by terrorists slammed into the towers, and within hours both immense structures were destroyed. There was nothing left but rubble and a few precariously leaning girders. Everything else had been crushed and pulverized.

Not long afterward, the architects and engineers must have stood at the site in shock as their dream lay before them in ruins. After so much planning, so much effort, so many long nights and weekends, it must have been devastating to see it all end in such horror.

With a far deeper sense of loss, the Trinity wept as Their dream for Old Testament Israel lay in ruins. How very different it could have been. Israel lost sight of their purpose and their destiny.[20]

Because of Israel's failure, the Godhead's vision was now passed on to Jesus' disciples. The Twelve became the inheritors of the same vision that had been given to Israel, although it was divested of its geographic and national elements. Ellen White states, "The Saviour turned from them [Israel] to entrust to others . . . the work they had slighted. *God's glory must be revealed,* . . . the disciples were called to do the work that the Jewish leaders had failed to do"[21] (italics supplied).

Once again the universe must have been shocked at the people Heaven chose to be the foundation of the new movement. But from the twelve disciples the New Testament church was eventually established and, under the blessing of the Holy Spirit, expanded dramatically.

The apostle Paul wrote extensively about God's purpose for the early church, especially in the book of Ephesians. The apostle focused once again on the church's vital role in revealing God's glory. *"Unto him be glory in the church* by Christ Jesus throughout all ages, world without end" (Ephesians 3:21, KJV; italics supplied).

As powerful as the New Testament church was, it, too, eventually lost sight of the Godhead's vision. During the Dark Ages, it strayed far from truth and became entrenched in corruption. Slowly, over time, God used men like Wycliffe, Luther, Melancthon, Wesley, and others to recover crucial parts of the vision, piece by precious piece.

Then, in 1844, God touched the life of a sickly teenager from Portland, Maine, Ellen G. White, who barely had a fourth-grade education. Through her prophetic visions, He began presenting a system of truth, a series of insights that paved the way for His glory—His character of love—to become the central focus once again.

Ellen White wrote, "That which God purposed to do for the world through Israel, . . . He will finally accomplish through His church on earth today."[22] And again, God's "… purpose for His people today is the *same* that He had for Israel"[23] (italics supplied).

God delights in using any Christian in any denomination who is willing to partner with Him. He has dedicated and sincere followers today in many churches. There are spiritual giants throughout Christendom. We have to be very careful that we don't make the same mistake as ancient Israel in thinking that Seventh-day Adventists have an exclusive lock on God's blessings. God is not limited to Adventist walls. At the time of Jesus' birth, He utilized wise men from the east to honor His Son. The Lord is impartial, has no elite favorites, and works in unexpected ways.

Nonetheless, God has given the Seventh-day Adventist Church a unique, essential role to play at the end of earth's history. Acknowledging that God can and will use Christians from other denominations does not diminish the specialized calling of the Adventist Church in any way. With its many additional insights and understandings, the Adventist Church is supposed to take a leading role in fulfilling God's purposes. It is not truth alone that makes us useful to Heaven, but a willingness to integrate those truths into our lives and maintain a humble, servantlike mentality.

The roots of the Adventist Church go back in time far beyond 1844. *We are the inheritors of a dream that the Godhead has had since Old Testament times, of revealing Their glory to the world.* We have been given the same fundamental charter that God gave to ancient Israel, adapted to the times in which we live.

Central to the truths that God has given our church are the three angels' messages of Revelation 14:6–12. The first angel's message states, "And I saw another angel fly in the midst of heaven, having the *everlasting gospel* to preach unto them that dwell on the earth, and to every nation, and kindred, and tongue, and people, / Saying with a loud voice, *Fear [honor] God,* and *give glory to him;* for the hour of his judgment is come: and *worship him* that made heaven, and earth, and the sea, and the fountains of waters" (Revelation 14:6, 7, KJV; italics supplied).

The "everlasting gospel" is first and foremost the good news about God. The verse goes on to say that we should honor Him, give glory to Him, and worship Him. It also calls attention to the judgment in heaven and the Sabbath as key elements in understanding God's desires and purposes. *The heart of our message and mission is clearly the Godhead.*[24]

The second and third angels' messages strongly warn people not to follow spiritual falsehood or stray from the gospel. The fundamental issue is worshiping the true God or worshiping the beast that seeks to obscure Him.[25]

The first angel's message tells us who God *is,* and the second and third angels' messages tell us who God *is not.* That is why Ellen White makes such a strong statement about what the primary burden of our message should be: "It is the darkness of misapprehension of God that is enshrouding the world. Men are losing their knowledge of His character. . . . Into the darkness of the world is to be shed the light of His glory, the light of His goodness, mercy, and truth.

". . . The last rays of merciful light, the last message of mercy to be given to the world, *is a revelation of His character of love*"[26] (italics supplied).

There are many parallels between God's expectations of Old Testament Israel and what He hopes will happen through the Adventist Church today.[27] Just as He did for ancient Israel, God has provided us with incredible understanding in many areas of life. Through the inspired writings of Ellen White, the Holy Spirit has given us specific insights regarding biblical truth, intellectual development, loving relationships, education, family, health, finance, service—*to enable us to portray the multifaceted dimensions of the Trinity.*

Just as God designed for ancient Israel, as a result of His guidance and grace the Seventh-day Adventist Church is to be renowned throughout the world.

When hearts long to understand Scripture; when corporate America looks for great leaders; when businesses seek exceptional employees; when organizations attempt to find people who will take on dirty, thankless tasks; when hurting, broken people need unconditional acceptance and care; when TV stations want to do specials on strong marriages and families; when industry scans the globe for innovation and creative genius; when *Time* magazine does a special on uniquely healthy lifestyles, the name "Seventh-day Adventist" should come immediately to mind. Our ranks should be filled with Mother Teresas, Einsteins, Churchills, and Mozarts. Most of all, our abundance of truth should lead to an abundance of love.

God's extraordinary blessings in us are to call attention back to Him as the Source. All the privileges we have been given are undeserved gifts of divine grace and should result in heartfelt praise.

Down through the centuries the Trinity's vision has been passed from Israel to the New Testament church, and now to God's remnant in the end time. It has been the same basic plan throughout the ages. We are told, "*From the beginning* it has been God's plan that through His church shall be reflected to the world His fullness and His sufficiency. The members of the church, those whom He has called out of darkness into His marvelous light, are to show forth His glory"[28] (italics supplied).

Now, after so many centuries of hope and bitter disappointment, the Trinity is looking with longing for people who will finally cooperate wholeheartedly in the fulfillment of Their momentous vision. It is a privilege and responsibility that should grip our souls. It calls us to participate in the most important endeavor of our day, far more important than what is happening in the halls of Congress or the New York Stock Exchange.

In Revelation 18:1, a fourth angel appears with a very hopeful message, foreseeing the time when God's glory and love will, indeed, encompass the globe: "And after these things I saw another angel come down from heaven, having great power; and the earth was lightened with his glory." The Godhead's dream will, at last, be wonderfully fulfilled.

---

1 See Ellen G. White, *The Desire of Ages,* p. 762.
2 See Ellen G. White, *Education,* p. 34.
3 See Ellen G. White, *The Story of Redemption*, p. 112.
4 See Exodus 33:18, 19.
5 See Ellen G. White, *Christ's Object Lessons*, p. 286.
6 See Deuteronomy 28:1; Ellen G. White, *Christ's Object Lessons*, p. 286.
7 See Ellen G. White, *Christ's Object Lessons,* p. 286; Isaiah 56:6–8; 58:1–12.
8 *The Seventh-day Adventist Bible Commentary*, 4:28; Ellen G. White, *Patriarchs and Prophets,* p. 378; Ellen G. White, *Christ's Object Lessons,* p. 288.
9 See Exodus 31:2–6; Ellen G. White, *Christ's Object Lessons,* p. 288; Exodus 35:30–35.
10 See Deuteronomy 30:9; Isaiah 51:3; Ellen G. White, *Christ's Object Lessons,* p. 289.
11 See Malachi 3:8–11; *The Seventh-day Adventist Bible Commentary*, 4:28.
12 See Isaiah 27:6; 51:3.
13 See Deuteronomy 7:6–15; Ellen G. White, *Patriarchs and Prophets,* pp. 378, 379; Ellen G. White, *Christ's Object Lessons*, p. 288; *The Seventh-day Adventist Bible Commentary*, 4:27.
14 See Ellen G. White, *Prophets and Kings,* pp. 292, 372, 487.
15 See Deuteronomy 28:13; Ellen G. White, *Christ's Object Lessons,* p. 288.
16 Ibid., p. 290.
17 Ibid., pp. 285, 286.
18 Ibid., p. 292.
19 "Revitalization of Lower Manhattan: The World Trade Center," http://www.unc.edu/courses/2001fall/plan/006e/001/project/chap1.html (public access forbidden).
20 See Ellen G. White, *Christ's Object Lessons*, p. 291.
21 Ellen G. White, *The Acts of the Apostles,* p. 16; see also Ellen G. White, *Christ's Object Lessons,* p. 296.
22 Ellen G. White, *Prophets and Kings,* p. 713.
23 Ellen G. White, *Counsels to Parents, Teachers, and Students,* p. 321.
24 See *Seventh-day Adventists Believe* … (Washington, D.C.: Ministerial

Association, General Conference of Seventh-day Adventists, 1988), pp. 144, 164; *The Seventh-day Adventist Bible Commentary*, 7-A:979.

25 See Revelation 14:9; *Seventh-day Adventists Believe . . .*, p. 167.

26 Ellen G. White, *Christ's Object Lessons,* p. 415.

27 See Ellen G. White, *Christ's Object Lessons,* p. 305.

28 Ellen G. White, *The Acts of the Apostles,* p. 9.

Chapter 3

Trinity Life

At 8:04 A.M. the commuter train sped south toward Cape Cod, Massachusetts, with seventy-four business people and tourists on board. Shortly before 8:06 A.M. it passed through the small rural town of Middleboro, a few seconds ahead of schedule. The train crossed over the bridge at Red River Bay at a few seconds past 8:11 A.M. People in the passenger cars gazed casually through the oversized, rectangular windows at the morning sun glistening on the water. A mild current was causing yachts in a marina to strain slightly at their tethers. At precisely 8:19 A.M., the fast-moving lead engine was parallel with the switching signal just outside the Cataumet Station, hurrying to its destination farther inland.

Suddenly the massive locomotive hit an obstacle on the tracks, dislodging the front wheels from the rail. The other six wheels quickly jumped the track in succession. All five passenger cars followed suit. As the train careened down a steep embankment, it fell heavily onto its left side and carved out a long, deep furrow littered with contorted metal and horribly mangled bodies.

Actually, the crash never happened. This is how I envisioned it happening in my five-year-old imagination as a result of my placing a nickel on the railroad tracks. We kids had placed pennies on the tracks many times before to be flattened by a train. We never gave it a second thought. But pennies are very thin.

On this morning, Charlie Fuller had dared me to put down a big fat nickel. No one had ever done that before. It was unknown territory, uncharted waters. I strongly resisted. He followed up with a double dare. I gritted my teeth and resisted again. Then he spoke the dreaded "triple dare." I had to comply or be labeled for life.

Later, as I sat on a nearby ridge waiting, I was filled with growing dread and decided this new experiment was way too dangerous. I was headed down to retrieve the five-cent piece when the train suddenly appeared not far up the track to my right. It was too late. I knew there would be a terrible crash and I would be put on trial for mass murder. "But, judge, it was a triple dare . . ."

To my everlasting relief the entire train passed by without incident, smashing my coin en route. I smiled up at Charlie with the swagger of a proven daredevil.

The Cataumet train station, site of this nerve-wracking episode, figures prominently in my heritage. I grew up directly across from this unassuming brick building with the slate roof and large double doors. My friends and I reenacted countless arrivals and departures on its main platform. My mother operated a bake shop out of the building for a time.

Most important, my grandfather, whom I never knew, was station agent there in the 1930s. Nanny told me about him. She also recounted how he died in her arms from massive internal bleeding at the age of fifty-five. Any writing genes I possess most likely come from him. He filled journals with poems during lulls in his hectic schedule. My favorite is about his deep commitment to Jesus Christ. His handsome, mustached face stares out at me from the one precious, faded picture we have of him on duty in his striped, coal-stained coveralls and cap, leaning against a luggage cart.

As an adult, I always stopped by that abandoned station whenever I was in the area. It is a direct link to special people, now deceased, who were family to me.

Even though I live many states away now and cannot easily return, I often go to the railroad station in my mind. My sister sent me a book of old photos of our town published by the local historical society. In it are several pictures of the railroad station I had never seen before, with accompanying text. I peruse it periodically at breakfast.

You see, I don't want to ever forget those vital roots. Forgetting would cast me adrift. Forgetting would be way too disorienting. Going there helps me get centered and reminds me who I am. It reduces the complexity of life down to its essential, fundamental elements.

Churches need to visit their roots often, as well. In order to be clear about their identity and stay centered, they frequently need to go back and revisit the places in Scripture that define who they are. Congregations need to reconnect often with what the Bible gives as the reason for their existence. Otherwise they can become disoriented and drift from their God-given purpose.

Unfortunately the one aspect of their biblical background that churches need to remember most is also the one that is usually the least talked about or least understood. In Scripture the church is supposed to find its identity and reason for existence in the Trinity. It is intended to model its very life after the Godhead. *Church life is supposed to be a reflection of Trinity life.*

Suppose you hung around the Godhead for a couple of months. You watched, listened, and took notes about Their relationship with each Other, Their relationships with created beings, and Their values and priorities. It is those very same kinds of relationships, values, and priorities that are to characterize the local church. We might illustrate this with the following graphic:

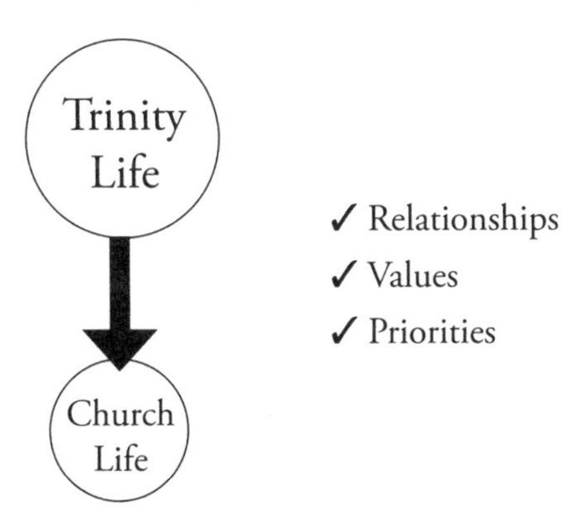

During the first thirty years of my life as an Adventist, the doctrine of the Trinity was one of those biblical truths that I was aware of but kept tucked away in a mental drawer and rarely, if ever, used, like a high-school graduation picture. I didn't learn very much about the Godhead in school. The subject mostly showed up in passing while we were studying something else. I don't ever remember hearing a sermon on the subject. I only recently discovered that there are entire books on that theme.

As Charles MacKenzie has observed: "Speculations about the Trinity seem irrelevant to citizens struggling for survival on a planet torn by internecine brush wars, threats of nuclear holocaust, and impending famine. Even involved church people, wrapped up in fund raising drives, ecclesiastical reorganizations, social service projects and study programs, have little awareness of the significance of the Trinity for their world."[1]

If I were the devil and wanted to derail the local church, to keep it struggling, I'd make sure the members didn't pay much attention to the doctrine of the Trinity. I would make them think it was too convoluted a subject to deal with. And if they did for some reason get interested in the topic, I'd make sure they didn't connect it at all to church life.

One of the most famous stories to come out of World War II was the sinking of the German ship *Bismarck*. It was described as the "greatest warship ever built, with guns so powerful and accurate it could destroy an enemy ship while safely staying outside the line of fire. The Allies had to *sink* it . . . or risk losing the war."[2]

After sea trials, the *Bismarck* left port on May 19, 1941, with the mission of attacking Allied shipping between Halifax, Nova Scotia, and Great Britain. Fully aware of the ominous threat posed by this titan of the seas, the British dispatched the most prized ship in the English navy, the HMS *Hood*, along with the *Prince of Wales*, to intercept her.[3]

They caught up with the *Bismarck* on May 24, and after a relatively brief battle, the *Hood*, symbol of British sea power, was blown up by a fifteen-inch shell that penetrated the hull and ignited the ship's ammunition magazine. The vessel sank almost immediately, taking with her 1,415 sailors. The news shook all of England.

The *Bismarck* left the scene, and an all-out search was initiated to find the elusive foe. Two days later, on May 26 at approximately 9:00 P.M., a British Swordfish biplane, launched from the aircraft carrier *Ark Royal*, spotted the ship. As darkness approached, the pilot dropped a single torpedo that sped toward the hulking behemoth. Normally such a torpedo would have minimal effect, but in what became known as the "miracle hit," it smashed into the *Bismarck*'s rudder and steering mechanism, crippling her at sea.[4] The largest, most powerful warship on the Atlantic had been rendered helpless by a single aircraft.

Able only to steam in a large circle, the German battleship became an easy target. The HMS *King George V* and the *Rodney*, two frontline British battleships, hurried to the scene. On Tuesday morning, May 27, about 9:00 A.M., both ships opened fire. After an hour and a half of intense shelling, the *Bismarck*'s guns fell silent. At 10:39 A.M. the *Bismarck* sank beneath the waves in three miles of water off the coast of Brest, France.[5]

The rudder is such a small thing, and yet so vital. By destroying it, the British destroyed an entire battleship.

In a similar way, the devil knows that in order to render the church ineffective today, all he has to do is target our ability to steer. Our rudder is the vision, the plan that the Godhead has had for the church since its very inception—*to reflect the life of the Trinity.* By getting us to lose sight of that vision, the devil removes our ability to move forward effectively. By absorbing our attention with lesser spiritual themes, Satan cripples our ability to fulfill God's purpose.

Millard J. Erickson observes, "The doctrine of the Trinity is crucial for Christianity. It is concerned with who God is, what he is like, how he works, and how he is to be approached."[6]

Stanley Grenz highlights both the complexity and centrality of this foundational Bible teaching: "Of the various aspects of our Christian understanding of God perhaps none is as difficult to grasp as the concept of God as triune. At the same time, no dimension of the Christian confession is closer to the heart of the mystery of God we have come to know. In fact, what sets Christianity apart from the other religious traditions is the confession that the one God is Father, Son, and Spirit. As a consequence, no teaching lies at the center of Christian theology, if not of Christian faith itself, as does the doctrine of the Trinity."[7]

We believe that God is made up of three fully equal, divine Persons—Father, Son, and Holy Spirit. They have no beginning and no end. Christianity is *monotheistic,* because the Members of the Godhead are One in nature, character, and purpose. We do not worship three separate gods. The Three Members of the Trinity are distinct from each Other within the one divine union we call "God."[8]

The doctrine of the Trinity is indicated in various places in the Old Testament. The name frequently used for God is *Elohim,* which is a plural.[9]

At the creation of this world we find that all the Members of the Godhead were involved in the process. Notice the plurals Moses uses in describing the creation of Adam and Eve: "And God said, Let *us* make man in *our* image, after *our* likeness" (Genesis 1:26, KJV; italics supplied).

In the New Testament, the Godhead is revealed much more explicitly. Take, for example, the announcement to Mary of Jesus' conception and birth. "The angel's testimony to Mary clearly indicates the activities of all [Members of the Trinity] in the mystery of God becoming man. ' "The *Holy Spirit* will come upon you, and the power of *the Highest* will overshadow you; therefore, also, that Holy One who is to be born will be called the *Son of God*" '(Luke 1:35)."[10]

The Members of the Godhead are mentioned at the Savior's baptism: "... when He had been baptized, [*Jesus*] came up immediately from the water; and behold, the heavens were opened to Him, and He saw the *Spirit of God* descending like a dove and alighting upon Him. And suddenly a voice came from heaven saying, 'This is *My* beloved Son, in whom I am well pleased' " (Matthew 3:16, 17, NKJV; italics supplied).

The Great Commission is another clear statement. " 'Go therefore and make disciples of all the nations, baptizing them in the name of the *Father and of the Son and of the Holy Spirit*' " (Matthew 28:19, NKJV; italics supplied).

Paul ends several of his letters by talking about the Three Members of the Godhead. For example, "The grace of the Lord *Jesus Christ,* and the love of *God,* and the communion of the *Holy Spirit* be with you all" (2 Corinthians 13:14, NKJV; italics supplied).

Because the Godhead is a "Tri-unity," They have chosen to create a plural entity called the church to represent Them. Just as one flower cannot be a bouquet; just as one note cannot be a symphony; so it is that no one person can reveal the Trinity. The Godhead is so loving, so complex, so amazing, that it takes entire congregations to begin to reflect who They are.

Have you seen what happens at a sports stadium when the spectators form a huge picture? As each one enters the stadium they are given a one-foot-square card with some kind of design or squiggles on it. If they looked at it they wouldn't have a clue what it meant. They are told, "At the signal, hold your card up like this," and someone demonstrates. After everyone is seated, the signal is given, and ten thousand people all hold their cards up together. And if you get back far enough you can suddenly see a picture of some famous person.

In a similar way, if, by the grace of God, we can offer up our everyday life in dedication and combine it with the lives of other members, people can begin to see something of God's glory. The church is also like a wonderful diamond, with each of us as one of the many sparkling facets that together reflect the Father, Son, and Holy Spirit.

The close connection between the Trinity and the church is highlighted in several places in Scripture. I will mention a few. The first reference is in the creation of Adam and Eve.

When human beings were brought into existence, the Bible tells us, "So God created man in *his own image*, in the image of God created he him; *male and female created he them*" (Genesis 1:27, KJV; italics supplied). It is vital to realize that it took *both* Adam and Eve *together* to reflect the image of God. Gilbert Bilezikian observes, "Since God is Trinity, he is plurality in oneness. Therefore, the creation in his image required the creation of a plurality of persons. God's supreme achievement was not the creation of a solitary man, but the creation of human community."[11]

This truth establishes a principle, a pattern with important implications for the church. The church's calling to reveal God is a call to community. It is only in our life together that God can truly be seen.

The famous Old Testament text most quoted by faithful Israelites was "Hear, O Israel: The LORD our God is one LORD" (Deuteronomy 6:4, KJV). The Hebrew word used for "one" in this verse is *'echad,* which means "one among others in a joined or shared oneness," referring again to the plurality within the Godhead.[12] Strikingly, that is the same word used in Genesis 2:24, NKJV, where we read, "Therefore a man shall leave his father and mother and be joined to his wife, and they shall become *one* flesh" (italics supplied).[13] It was to reflect this "shared oneness" within the Trinity that the nation of Israel was created.

The connection between the Godhead and the church is more fully developed in several places in the New Testament. Most compelling is Jesus' amazing prayer just hours before He died. It was, in effect, His "last will and testament." Because His life was ending, He undoubtedly chose His words very carefully.

Christ and His disciples had just left the upper room and were making their way down into the Kidron Valley toward Gethsemane. The full moon shone from a clear, cloudless sky. He taught along the way, urging the Twelve to love one another as He had loved them (see John 15:12). Then, at some point, the Savior stopped His instruction to His followers, turned His eyes toward the heavens, and poured out the burden of His heart.

With His disciples gathered around in awed silence, He spoke to His Father. " 'I do not pray for these alone, *but also for those who will believe in Me through their word*' " (John 17: 20, NKJV; italics supplied). The focus of Christ's petition was not only His disciples but the church down through time, including us today.

As the Lord continued, He made a remarkable statement regarding the church: " 'Holy Father, protect them by the power of your name . . .

that they may be one *as we are one*' " (John 17:11, NIV; italics supplied). Did you catch those last four words? *"As we are one."* Jesus longs for the relationships within the church to be modeled after the relationships within the Trinity itself! Millard Erickson writes, "The perfect love and unity within the Godhead model for us the oneness and affection that should characterize our relationships within the body of Christ."[14]

The apostle Paul also talked about the relationship between the Trinity and the church, especially in the book of Ephesians. The Members of the Godhead are the central Characters throughout the epistle. Chapter 1 refers to the Father, Jesus Christ, and the Holy Spirit, and it recounts how it was through Their combined efforts that the church was created (see Ephesians 1:3–14). Through Them we are blessed, chosen, redeemed, and sealed. They are intimately involved with the entire makeup of the church. Reflecting on these verses, John R. W. Stott concludes, "Christian faith and Christian life are both fundamentally trinitarian."[15]

In Ephesians 2, the apostle compares the New Testament church to a temple. Unlike the Jewish sanctuary of the Old Testament, this one is being constructed with people rather than stones. It is a spiritual building. Paul says that this human temple is the dwelling place for the Trinity: "In [Christ] the whole building is joined together and rises to become a holy temple in the *Lord.* And in him you too are being built together *to become a dwelling in which God lives by his Spirit*" (Ephesians 2:21, 22, NIV; italics supplied). The Godhead is no longer manifest in the Shekinah glory of Israel's sanctuary but is to be evidenced, rather, in the relationships and quality of life among Their followers who make up the new temple, the church.[16]

And finally, the opening verses of Ephesians 4 talk about the sevenfold oneness that should characterize the church. Three of these unities specifically refer to the Members of the Trinity. The remaining four refer to the believer's relationship with the Father, Son, and Holy Spirit. "There is one body and *one Spirit,* just as you were called in one hope of your calling; *one Lord,* one faith, one baptism; *one God and Father* of all" (Ephesians 4:4–6, NKJV; italics supplied). Once again the Three Members of the Godhead are central to the life of the church and interwoven in it.

Charles MacKenzie summarizes the nature of the relationships within the Godhead that are to be emulated in the church: "The Biblical record teaches that within the unity of God there eternally have existed three Lovers. . . . It is one personality reaching out to another personality in a special relationship. . . . The three love each other so intensely that they are bound together in an eternal and indissoluble oneness. . . . Their oneness in love coalesces their thoughts, wills, feelings, consciousness, and power into perfect harmony. Their mutual love is the perfect community for which all people yearn."[17]

Even though the doctrine of the Trinity is essential, it took many years for early church leaders to define its meaning. Through lengthy gatherings and heated debates, a document eventually was hammered out in the fourth century that contained the foundational concepts on which the church is built.

In some ways the difficult process of finding consensus on the Trinity was similar to what our forefathers experienced in developing the American Constitution. George Washington was greatly agitated. Pacing the halls of his beloved home, Mount Vernon, he doubted that the Constitutional Convention scheduled for May 25, 1787, at the Philadelphia State House would amount to very much at all. Aching with rheumatism, downcast over the loss of a brother, and distracted by the management of his sprawling estate, Washington delayed his decision to go. The great leader also questioned whether very many men of stature would attend. Finally, after months of wavering, he agreed to be present.

Overall, seventy-four delegates from the thirteen states were invited, but only fifty-five actually attended. Rhode Island's leaders boycotted because they perceived it to be a conspiracy to overthrow the existing government. Thomas Jefferson and Samuel Adams were overseas. Without doubt the most notable attendee was the eighty-one year old Benjamin Franklin, hobbled by gout. The youngest person there was twenty-seven-year-old Jonathan Dayton, from New Jersey. Most of the delegates were well versed in law and philosophical theories of government. In spite of the absence of some key leaders, the convention was, nonetheless, an exceptionally learned gathering.

The sessions were held in secret with no reporters or visitors allowed, which only served to fuel suspicions. Thomas Jefferson wrote from Paris, "I am sorry they began their deliberations by so abominable a precedent as that of tying up the tongues of their members."[18]

As the days progressed, tensions mounted. At issue was whether or not to strengthen the role of the federal government—whether or not to broaden the powers of national leadership. Distrust of federal authority ran so deep that a series of newspaper articles appeared that summer alleging that a plot was under way to install the second son of George III, Frederick, Duke of York, to be "king of the United States."

In the early days of the nation, the federal government was intentionally designed to have limited power. It was now obvious to many that the weakness of the central government had put the various states on the brink of economic ruin. Commerce was severely depressed. Inflation was rampant. Small farmers were in especially dire straights, with many languishing in jail for not paying their debts, while their farms were being confiscated and sold for taxes. The issues were crucial. Something had to be done. But what?

Various plans and theories were submitted and hotly debated—the Virginia Plan, the New Jersey Plan, and Hamilton's proposal. By late June, debate between the large and small states over the issue of representation in the legislature became increasingly rancorous. With the speeches degenerating into intimidation and accusations, Benjamin Franklin pleaded for daily prayers. One member later stated that the convention "was on the verge of dissolution, scarce held together by the strength of a hair."

Finally, by mid-September, utter weariness and the desire to return home overcame any lingering wrangling. On September 15, the Constitution of the United States received a majority vote. Ben Franklin appealed for unity behind the precious document and declared, "I think it will astonish our enemies, who are waiting with confidence to hear that our councils are confounded like those of the builders of Babel."[19]

The Constitution, as we all know, is the foundation of our nation, the north star of our society. The highest court in the land is charged with making sure it is followed. Just recently the Supreme Court told President George W. Bush that a detention program he initiated had to be abandoned because it was "unconstitutional." If it does not line up with the Constitution, it cannot be done.

A similar lengthy, deliberative process took place with regard to the development of the doctrine of the Trinity during the fourth century A.D. Consensus on the subject did not come easily. Various factions vied strenuously for their opinion. Questions loomed. Was Christ created or not? Was He truly human, or did He simply appear to be human? What was the role of the Holy Spirit? If God the Father, Christ, and the Holy Spirit are all divine, how can we still say we worship one God? The church was torn.

Like the Constitutional Convention of 1787, a decision was made to convene a special meeting to consider the matter. The Council of Nicaea met in A.D. 325 with more than three hundred church leaders in attendance. The opposing theories of Alexander and Arius, in particular, were hotly debated. Significant progress was made but critical issues remained, especially the role of the Holy Spirit. Fifty-six years later, in A.D. 381, another council was called in Constantinople. Finally, after another round of debates, charges and countercharges, a document emerged that expounds the Christian understanding of the Godhead.[20]

As Adventists we "do not accept the Trinitarian formula based on the authority of church dogma or of church councils, but on the fact that it best represents what Scripture presents."[21] The document that emerged in A.D. 381 served a valuable function, however, by pointing the way toward the biblical answers.

The doctrine of the Trinity should be the spiritual constitution for every Seventh-day Adventist church—the standard, the north star. The true measure of a church's success is the extent to which its teachings, life, and ministry reveal the truth about the Trinity. Any values and priorities of the local church that do not harmonize with those of the Godhead must be discarded.

Life within the Trinity has many dimensions. *The following chapters will explore some of those dimensions and their meaning for the church today.* There is no more important or fascinating topic than the life that is shared by the Father, Son, and Holy Spirit. No subject is more central to the mission of Seventh-day Adventists who are called to reveal God's glory, no theme more critical to our success in the eyes of Heaven.

The relationships, values, and priorities that characterize the Godhead are worthy of our best thinking and most careful investigation. The remainder of this book seeks to take us a few steps further on that all-important journey.

---

1 Charles Sherrard MacKenzie, *The Trinity and Culture* (New York: Peter Lang Publishing, 1987), p. 63.

2 Quoted from "Synopses and Reviews," *The Deadly Hunt,* by William L. Shirer at http://www.powells.com/biblio?isbn=1402731833, Nov. 22, 2006; italics in original.

3 http://home.mem.net/~dalrympl/Bismarck.html, Nov. 22, 2006.

4 http://en.wikipedia.org/wiki/German_battleship_Bismarck, Nov. 22, 2006.

5 http://home.mem.net/~dalrympl/Bismarck.html, Nov. 22, 2006.

6 Millard J. Erickson, *Christian Theology* (Grand Rapids, Mich.: Baker Book House, 1985), p. 322.

7 Stanley J. Grenz, *Theology for the Community of God* (Nashville, Tenn.: Broadman & Holman, 1994), p. 69.

8 Woodrow Whidden, Jerry Moon, and John W. Reeve, *The Trinity* (Hagerstown, Md.: Review and Herald® Publishing Association, 2002), p. 20.

9 See Gerald Bray, *The Doctrine of God* (Downers Grove, Ill.: InterVarsity Press, 1993), p. 140; Donald Macleod, *Shared Life: The Trinity and the Fellowship of God's People* (Tain, Ross-shire, Scotland: Christian Focus Publications, 1994), p. 12.

10 *Seventh-day Adventists Believe . . .* (Washington, D.C.: General Conference Ministerial Association, 1988, First Edition), p. 24.

11 Gilbert Bilezikian, *Community 101* (Grand Rapids, Mich.: Zondervan, 1997), p. 19.

12 *The Trinity and Culture*, pp. 33, 34.

13 Ibid.

14 *Christian Theology*, p. 342.

15 John R. W. Stott, *The Message of Ephesians: God's New Society* (Downers Grove, Ill.: InterVarsity Press, 1979), p. 52.

16 Ibid., pp. 108, 109.

17 *The Trinity and Culture*, pp. 72, 81.

18 Adapted from "A More Perfect Union: The Creation of the U.S. Constitution" at the U.S. National Archives & Records Administration Web site: http://www.archives.gov/national-archives-experience/charters/print_friendly.html?page=constitution_history_content.html&title=NARA%20%7C%20The%20Constitution%20of%20the%20United%20States%3A%20A%20History, December 21, 2006.

19 Ibid.

20 See *The Trinity and Culture*, pp. 135–148.

21 *The Trinity and Culture*, p. 150.

Chapter 4

Creativity

By the time I was five or six years old I owned a house, a store, a moon rocket, a time machine, and a yacht. Most of them were made from refrigerator boxes. When refrigerator sales in town slumped, I simply threw a few blankets over the dining-room table and crawled underneath instead. I also worked as a conductor on a passenger train by riding back and forth a zillion times on a backyard swing set.

One memorable day my dad came home with an incredible gift—a large box full of odds and ends of leftover lumber from a construction site. Man! My eyes didn't see lumber, they saw towers and cars and fire houses and castles and bus stations.

That next Christmas I was given a real, honest-to-goodness lab burner that could produce an open flame. For some reason, during the summer I became obsessed with discovering what would happen if I heated up rocks. So, for two months I roamed the countryside looking for pieces of granite, shale, sandstone, and other samples to hold over the fire and expertly analyze.

A couple of years later, I abandoned my old cardboard winter home and moved into the summer cottage that a friend and I built in the fork of two huge limbs in a catalpa tree. We hoisted up scrap boards and hammered together a floor, four odd-sized walls, a roof, and a fairly functional door with two hinges.

In a building frenzy worthy of a caffeine-infused beaver, a gang of us also journeyed about a hundred yards down the railroad tracks and built several forts from small trees and green bows that we lashed together with twine. Top-secret meetings within the forts covered a diverse agenda from exploring various techniques for making gross noises to devising elaborate World War II battle plans. Sticks became rifles. Pine cones became grenades.

That was in the mid-1950s, and many years have passed. Now, for me, refrigerator boxes remain refrigerator boxes, and pieces of lumber look like pieces of lumber. Wonder, creativity, and imagination are such a large part of our early years, but, sadly, those qualities too often fade away when we become adults. Reality sets in. Responsibilities multiply. We get very busy with myriad tasks that absolutely must get done as soon as possible.

That is what usually happens. For Christians, however, that need not be true at all. We don't want to retreat into immature childishness, but from a spiritual point of view there is no reason that creativity and imagination cannot grow with us and, rather than fading, deepen and expand with age.

As I began to study the biblical concept that the church is to reflect the life of the Trinity, I came to realize that such a life would have to include creativity. If I were to make a list of the most prominent characteristics of the Godhead, creativity would certainly be near the top. And if it is such an important part of who God is, then it needs to be an important part of who we are, as well.

Because we are made in the image of God, we all have the privilege of being called to a life of creativity. "But I don't have a creative bone in my body," someone protests. In 2 Corinthians the apostle Paul gives us some great news when he writes, "Therefore, if any one is in Christ, *he is a new creation;* the old has passed away, behold, the new has come" (2 Corinthians 5:17, RSV; italics supplied). Through the creative power of the indwelling Christ you have been given new life. And if Jesus lives in you, His creativity is within you, as well. *You are a creative person!* [1] Sin may have terribly stifled and stunted our creativity, but as part of our spiritual restoration it can be re-discovered and enjoyed.

When Jesus walked this earth, creativity was in every fiber of His being. Taking the divine Being who was at the center of creating the entire universe and incarnating Him into our sinful, change-resistant world was bound to cause a tumultuous reaction. And it did.

Society, especially religious society, could only stand Him for three and a half years. He brought too many new ways of thinking. Too many new values and perspectives. Too many new associations and behaviors.

I am convinced that if Christ was incarnated in our own day, a number of church members would again feel He was introducing too many radical ideas into our churches. He would once again be accused of spending too much time hanging around the wrong people. He would again revolutionize, instigate, and irritate. Can we really expect anything different from the One who was the greatest change Agent the world has ever seen? I can envision some churches disfellowshiping Him.

Who else but Jesus would have thought of choosing such a motley group of twelve men to be the foundation of the New Testament church? He didn't follow the norm by gathering a safe, sedate, predictable band of scholarly disciples. He went way outside the box and made stunningly bold choices, including teenagers, several uneducated fishermen, a despised tax collector, and a couple of nationalistic fanatics. The Savior was able to select those kinds of people because He knew He could recreate them.

Jesus was wonderfully creative as a Teacher. In the Sermon on the Mount, He demonstrated a remarkable ability to see old, familiar scriptures in a brand-new way. He used a great variety of methods to express Himself, including personification, analogy, and hyperbole. He painted word pictures and immortalized mundane daily events by giving them a creative spin. He could make up parables on the spot, and we have more than forty of them.

I attended seminary from 1971 to 1973. The teaching styles varied from straight lecture to interactive. My favorite professor brought doughnuts and cider to class. Another professor walked up and down among the desks as he talked, animatedly throwing his whole body into the task, whirling around, punching the air, nodding his head, leaning on students' desks, pacing up front. The man was in shape!

On the very boring side of the ledger, I vividly remember an elderly professor who must have been steeped in the classical European pedagogical method. I hope he was beyond his prime. Great content but zero energy. We'd all file into this large auditorium for class. At the precise hour indicated on the schedule, he would march on stage unsmiling from the wings. He usually took ten steps horizontally then turned at a ninety-degree angle to the left and took two more steps to arrive at the ponderous podium.

"Stiff" does not quite capture the severity of his posture. The sharply carved white mustache that adorned his upper lip was about the size and shape of a small Band-Aid. The few white sprigs that sat atop his head appeared to have been placed with self-conscious care. He laid a large black three-ring notebook on the lectern and proceeded to read. Only his mouth moved, and he enunciated precisely. His eyes never strayed from the pages. When the bell rang for dismissal, he exited by executing the same angular movements in reverse order, disappearing stage left.

How different this professor's demeanor would have been if Jesus had been his model as a Teacher when he grew up! Stiffness would be gone. Boring would be gone. Rigor mortis movements would be gone. No more lecturing from pages yellowed with age. No more lifeless facts. He might even have made us laugh. Only a granite-hearted person could sit at Jesus' feet for very long and not be affected by His lively, energizing method of educating. He was creativity personified.

As Jesus' followers and representatives, our lives can be infused with creativity, as well, each of us expressing it in our own way. Learning how to manifest the creativity that was so central to the Savior's life is a valuable aspect of becoming His disciples.

Probably the greatest motivation in Scripture for recognizing and developing our creativity is to honor and glorify God. Giving Him glory means extolling who He is and what He has done.

I have often heard it said that the primary mission of the church is soul winning. Sharing the gospel is certainly very important, but it is not of first importance. As needy as humankind is, the primary focus of the Christian life and of the church should be directed toward bringing praise to God. Everything else grows out of that fundamental orientation. Glorifying Him infuses all else with authenticity and love.

Jesus taught, " 'By this my Father is glorified, that you bear much fruit' " (John 15:8, RSV). God is honored when we activate the talents and abilities we have been given. A teacher is honored by the accomplishments of his students. A master craftsman is honored by the dedication and skill evidenced in his intern.

The apostle Paul emphasized the same theme when he wrote, "So whether you eat or drink or whatever you do, do it all for the glory of God" (1 Corinthians 10:31, NIV). Giving glory to God is also at the heart of the first angel's message of Revelation 14:6, 7.

During medieval times artists did not sign their work. The only reason Michelangelo put his name on the famous *Pieta* was that he was incensed when people gave credit to others for his work. But later he regretted having signed his name. These individuals wanted their art to glorify the Master Designer who gifted them so abundantly, not to point toward themselves.[2]

Ray Stedman hits the nail on the head when he writes, "The first task of the church is not the welfare of human beings. Yes, our welfare is definitely important to God, but that is not the church's first task. Rather, we have been chosen by God to live to the praise and glory of God, so that through our lives His glory will be revealed to the world."[3]

Our living creatively in order to glorify God removes all self-interest and frees us from worrying about what others might think. It provides the greatest possible incentive for us to step outside our comfort zones, to make the attempt and to persist in order to cause the universe to more raucously praise the Father, Son, and Holy Spirit. Every time we choose creativity over the expected or the norm, we are honoring our Creator. Viewing creativity this way makes it a form of prayer and worship, an offering to our Lord.

Creative living is not typically something emphasized or taught in churches. Neither is it very often part of most people's self-image. *As a result, when we come into adulthood, we have several reasons why we may be reluctant to attempt creative things:*

1. The way we define creativity. We often have a hard time picturing ourselves as creative people because we think creativity is reserved only for "real" artists such as musicians, composers, painters, sculptors, and writers. Such a definition is far too limited and narrow. We need more expansive definitions like the following:

"... Creativity is the ability to see things in a new way."[4]

"Being creative is seeing the same thing as everybody else but thinking of something different."[5]

Creativity is "the ability to take existing objects and combine them in different ways for new purposes."[6]

There ought to be enough space in those definitions for all of us to find a place for ourselves. Thinking differently, seeing things differently, finding fresh ways to put ordinary things together—that's doable. At its root, creativity is not first of all an activity but an attitude. It is an affirmation of who we are as redeemed people. It is trusting our calling. It is taking delight in our giftedness from God.

For the Christian, creativity can become *a way of life,* permeating our perspectives and behaviors. *It can include creative ways of* potty training a toddler, disciplining our children, fixing meals, decorating our home, problem-solving at work, managing a department, wrapping Christmas presents, reacting to hurt, showing affection, helping the poor, saving for retirement, managing our time, having family worship, planning vacations, keeping the Sabbath, and on and on. Not every activity needs to be infused with special creativity, but that mind-set can color our whole approach to life and be utilized as we have opportunity.

My wife, Ann, has always been a fine cook. A few years ago she had to find a way to lower her cholesterol, which launched her into a search for recipes short on fat and long on taste. It has become a delicious adventure for both of us. I never know what to expect when I arrive home from work. Last night we had healthy, out-of-this-world little pita-bread pizzas.[7] The night before that dinner included Pineapple-Potato Boats. If you asked her if she was creative, Ann would probably answer "No." But in my eyes her eagerness to try new recipes only can come from a wonderfully creative heart.

During a weekly church service, Pastor Davida Crabtree asked all of those who cut or styled people's hair professionally to come forward for a special prayer of dedication. Her hopeful, inspiring words capture well the spirit of creativity that can infuse all of life.

"Creator and creating God, we raise before You in prayer all who work as hairdressers, barbers, and beauticians, who by their creativity and skill seek to help people feel good about themselves. Be present to them and grant them patience in their many interactions with the public and co-workers. Grant them a sense of ministry in their listening to the lonely and hurting, in their ability to transform mundane interactions into meaningful relationships, in their ability to give joy and feelings of self-worth simply by their work. In the name of Jesus Christ, we pray. Amen."[8]

You might say, "But, Kim, I'm not imaginative enough to be creative." We actually use our imagination all the time just to function throughout the day. Without imagination we could not accomplish anything. Whether we are fixing breakfast or solving a complex problem, we first imagine ourselves doing it and then we do it.[9]

You have a great imagination. You just need to channel it in new ways.

2. We are afraid that we will fail. Our family rented the first floor of a house in the country. The sunroom had a whole wall of windows overlooking the side yard. One morning, as I gazed out toward the owner's extensive garden, I saw a large owl about thirty yards away perched atop a six-foot-high post. I hurriedly went and got my wife and daughter, and we all stared in delight.

We didn't have binoculars, so I suggested, "Why don't we go outside and see if we can get closer?" They agreed. So the three of us quietly headed out the front door, nervously tip-toed across the dirt driveway, and hid on the far side of the big red barn. I motioned for them to follow as I snuck carefully around to the corner. I stopped, leaned out slightly, and took a peek with one eye. The big bird was still sitting there.

Emboldened, I whispered, "Why don't we creep up on it and see how close we can *really* get?" We moved ahead stealthily once again. My heart pounded as we inched forward like Navy Seals on a mission. I thought, *What a great opportunity to see this beautiful creature up close in the daytime! My daughter will remember this forever.* We kept moving forward, knowing the bird could fly away at any moment.

Finally, when I was only fifteen feet away, I looked more carefully and then said, "Hey . . . this thing's a fake! Just a piece of carved wood." A feeling of horrible embarrassment suddenly washed over me. In a moment I went from Mr. Audubon to Bozo. We glanced around in all directions to see if anyone had witnessed the incident and then stood up straight and walked purposefully back to the house as if we were simply out on an early morning stroll.

I hate the kind of red-faced feeling that accompanies such misadventures. We all do. It is the feeling that comes when we make mistakes or mess up. Unfortunately, our desire to avoid that negative emotion can keep us from attempting new and creative adventures, projects, and endeavors. We wind up playing it safe.

In Jesus' parable of the talents, two of the men invested their money and were commended. Fearing failure, the third man took his windfall and buried it in the backyard. He wouldn't gain anything, but he wouldn't lose either. When the lord returned, it was the third man he berated. The lesson: It is better to have tried and failed than to have never tried at all. The following poem gets at Jesus' point:

> There was a very cautious man
> Who never laughed or played.

He never risked, he never tried,
He never sang or prayed.

And when one day he passed away
His insurance was denied,
For since he never really lived,
They claimed he never died.[10]

In order to free up our creativity, we need to abolish the word *failure* and substitute *learning experience.* That is especially true for the Christian. I read that weavers in India, when they make a mistake, don't discard the rug but simply incorporate the mistake into an even more beautiful design.[11] Our God is so wise that He can take all of our failed attempts and incorporate them into our lives in such a way that the final result is even more beautiful than if we had never tried at all.

3. We don't feel we have time to be creative. Our lives can become so frantic as we race from one responsibility to the next that creativity gets crowded out. People tend to do what they value; so, the best remedy is to alter our value system. Needless to say, maximum fulfillment and joy come when our values mirror God's. Besides, creativity does not need to be one more activity tacked on to an otherwise hectic day; it can simply be integrated into what we already do.

In order to live creatively we need to take time to nourish that aspect of our lives through reflection, study, exploration, practice, and experimentation. Such time is not "wasted." It is all part of glorifying God by bringing our frenetic lives more into balance. It is part of discovering fuller dimensions of ourselves.

Living creatively also is the most effective thing we can do to raise creative kids by modeling for them that it is a consistent priority.

During my pastoral years, when our daughter Stefanie was about three years old, she loved to hang around my study while I prepared a sermon. We eventually found a small desk she could call her own and gave her crayons and a stack of blank paper to scribble on.

When I opened a book, Stef did the same, although she often held it upside down because she was too young to read. She'd open some thick Bible commentary and stare up and down each page very studiously. She even put a bookmark in there when she had to go potty.

One day I heard a noise behind me as I was writing. I swiveled around and heard her say loudly, "Oh, shoot," then crumple up a piece of paper and toss it on the floor in front of her in disgust. I asked what she was doing, and she replied, "I'm making a sermon just like you."

Example is a powerful tool. Your sense of adventure and excitement over creative endeavors can inspire your children to put away the video games and take time to develop their own giftedness.

The topic of creativity has great importance not only for us as individuals but also for local congregations, as well. As Seventh-day Adventists we believe that Sabbath is a memorial of Creation. It is that to be sure. But more than that, it is a celebration of the creativity within the heart of God.[12] *Therefore, as an important part of their mission to reflect the life of the Trinity, churches need to highly value and actively foster innovation and creativity.* In fact, Adventist churches are called to be the most innovative, creative places on the planet.

Thomas G. Bandy, in his book *Kicking Habits*, provides a stirring synopsis of what a church might look like that understands the full dimensions of its call to creativity. The following are excerpts:

> The thriving church system is all about "changing." . . . The thriving church helps [people] to discern and use their spiritual gifts in surprising and unexpected ways. It assists them to explore their relationship with Christ, and to discover a personal and practical destiny, or calling. . . . [It] encourages individual initiative, self-discovery, and deep spirituality. . . . It will be an organization with an overarching sense of identity and purpose, but which allows the many parts of the organism . . . freedom to do what they were created to do. Such an organization will concentrate on motivating, communicating, and training,

> rather than controlling, coordinating, and initiating. . . . Therefore, the thriving church is radically diverse, and bursting with any number of activities or missions, involving all ages, cultures, languages, and races.[13]

Such a lively portrayal will be fulfilled by churches committed to revealing the heart of the Creator. It will emerge in churches that nurture a spirit of discovery by creating environments where people feel safe to experiment and fail. It will be realized through congregations that understand that their Lord was not only a profound Teacher and compassionate Healer, but also the most revolutionary, comfort zone–busting Person who ever lived.

From my experience, we have a ways to go. I have seen wonderful Adventist churches that embrace innovative ministries. I have also observed the sad things that happen when the vision fades. Fostering and pursuing creativity is essential because it reflects directly on the picture we are painting of God.

In light of God's mandate, it is unfortunate that so many of our churches across North America organize church life in such a cookie-cutter fashion and utilize such similar outreach methods. Rediscovering the central role of creativity within God's vision for the church can open up a whole host of powerful possibilities for Seventh-day Adventist congregations.

One of the spiritual gifts that God especially designed to help guide churches into new possibilities is the gift of faith as manifested in the visionaries among us. Visionaries, by definition, usually come from the edges of a paradigm and can sound unsettling as advocates of change. But it is at the edges of any living plant where growth occurs. Anyone can spot wrong answers, but visionaries specialize in recognizing wrong questions.

Visionaries may often be ignored simply because they are ahead of their time. When Yale University student Fred Smith submitted a paper proposing a reliable overnight delivery system, his management professor commented skeptically, " 'The concept is interesting and well-formed, but in order to earn better than a "C," the idea must be feasible.' "[14] Smith went on to be the founder of FedEx.

Churches that embrace the future will make time to teach leaders, boards, and committees how to think creatively. As a result, in their deliberations and planning, they will refuse to settle for either/or thinking but will rather opt for the genius of a both/and approach. "The idea is to put the 'ands' together, to combine seemingly contradictory things in creative ways that actually turn out better than they would have working apart. . . . Praying *and* planning . . . Doctrinal purity *and* cultural relevance."[15] These churches will also make teaching new members how to be creative an important part of their discipling process.

Creative churches will bring members who are part of what is often called "the arts" into the mainstream of church life. These are typically the composers, musicians, painters, sculptors, and writers among us. Their talent is focused on producing something tangible, something new or renewed, which is usually intended for others to see and experience. Because they are such an intense embodiment of God's creative Spirit, they deserve special honor.

In order to reach the masses of society, especially the youth, we need to channel many of our most creative minds into recapturing all types of media for Christ, including acting and film. If the Savior is to be Lord of all, it must include every aspect of our culture. We do not need to only produce overtly religious material. Through the arts we can build many bridges into the hearts and minds of non-Christians and speak to them in powerful ways by portraying stories and characters that focus on high moral values and priorities.

Steve Turner highlights how God can touch individuals through the arts in very poignant ways. "Many people are involved in working with art because they want to expand the quality of people's lives. Children whose lives have been blighted by war, famine or abuse are quite often reawakened by music, dance, poetry, painting and drama. Their senses are engaged. Their experience is enlarged. Their damaged 'Godlikeness' is allowed to reemerge, and often for the first time, they feel the wonder of being human." [16]

Our call to creativity is a call to joy and adventure. It is a call to stretch and grow as we seek to reflect the life of the One who brought all things into existence. It is an opportunity to manifest the spirit of our God who is constantly at work today, both within the church and without, attempting to re-create and renew. Elizabeth Barrett Browning's poem captures the contrast between eyes and hearts attuned to our Creator's workings and those who have yet to understand.

"Earth's crammed with heaven,
And every common bush afire with God;
But only he who sees takes off his shoes,
The rest sit round it and pluck blackberries."[17]

1 Adapted from Alice Bass, *The Creative Life* (Downers Grove, Ill.: InterVarsity Press, 2001), p. 27.

2 Michael Card, *Scribbling in the Sand: Christ and Creativity* (Downers Grove, Ill.: InterVarsity Press, 2002), pp. 78, 79.

3 Ray Stedman, *Body Life* (Grand Rapids, Mich.: Discovery House Publishers, 1995), p. 28.

4 Howard G. Hendricks, *Color Outside the Lines* (Nashville: W Publishing Group, 1998), p. 8.

5 http://members.optusnet.com.au/~charles57/Creative/Basics/definitions.htm, Dec. 20, 2006.

6 Ibid.

7 Cheryl Thomas Caviness, *Fabulous Food* (Hagerstown, Md.: Review and Herald®, 1990), p. x.

8 Quoted from Davida Foy Crabtree, *The Empowering Church* (Herndon, Va.: Alban Institute, 1989), p. 67.

9 Michael Card, *Scribbling in the Sand: Christ and Creativity*, p. 55.

10 Howard Hendricks, Quoted in *Color Outside the Lines,* p. 65.

11 Ibid., p. 66.

12 See Ellen G. White, *Education*, p. 250.

13 Thomas G. Bandy, *Kicking Habits* (Nashville: Abingdon Press, 2001), pp. 135–138.

14 Howard Hendricks, *Color Outside the Lines*, p. 4.

15 Ibid., p. 53.

16 Steve Turner, *Imagine: A Vision for Christians in the Arts* (Downers Grove, Ill.: InterVarsity Press, 2001), p. 84.

17 Quoted in *Color Outside the Lines,* p. 28; italics in original.

Chapter 5

Transcendence

My dear wife's eyes bugged out in disbelief as she stared at the herd of seventy-five fenced-in mules. We had reserved three of these tall critters months earlier, one each for me, my wife Ann, and our twelve-year-old daughter Stefanie, to ride with a tour group down into the Grand Canyon. Technically a mule is a cross between a horse and a donkey. From my wife's vantage point, they looked more like a cross between a horse and a warehouse. Stef and I had some riding experience, but my wife had never ridden anything.

Soon the caravan leader came over and assured her, "I've reserved the gentlest mule for you. She's as placid as they come . . . and you can ride right behind me." After further assurances and a few practice trots around the corral, we were on our way.

We descended in groups of eight down into the canyon's breathtaking depths on a trail no wider than a few skateboards. A rock wall rose on one side, and a sheer five-hundred-foot drop-off fell away on the other. The leader warned that when we stopped to rest we should always face our mules out toward the canyon. Otherwise they might get spooked by a snakey looking stick, back up too far, and prematurely meet their Maker.

As the mule train progressed, we discovered that these large animals relieve themselves in torrents. Being very fastidious, the mule that follows will not step in the other mule's pee. So, they tip-toe around it on the *outside,* every time.

On the way back I looked up ahead and saw the leader's mule rear up, just like in an old-time John Wayne western. We were immediately told to halt. Someone had spotted a real live rattlesnake just over the edge of the trail. While one ranger stood poised with rock in hand, another led us one by one past the nasty reptile. A little farther on, my famished mule spotted some leafy delicacy in the wilderness and bolted for an off-track snack.

Throughout the safari, my wife was very brave. Much braver than I first realized, because that evening she told us that bouncing on the saddle for six hours had created a painful, fist-sized raw area on her backside that took weeks to heal.

The all-day mule trek provided a unique view of the canyon that helped us appreciate more fully its immensity and grandeur. Looking up from the valley floor is absolutely riveting. The place is truly huge!

Since that visit, for me the Grand Canyon has become a kind of touchstone. When I lapse into small-mindedness and petty gripes, I often remember the mules and the stunning view. It paints me and my concerns on a much larger canvas. It has a humbling, calming effect and broadens my perspective.

Something similar, yet much more profound, happens when I consider the greatness of God. The Scriptures tell us, " 'How great you are, O Sovereign Lord! There is no one like you, and there is no God but you' " (2 Samuel 7:22, NIV).

God is what theologians call "transcendent." The Trinity transcends everything with which we are familiar. They are above and beyond every notion we have of life and its various dimensions.

The past, present, and future are equally open to the Godhead. That's why we read in Exodus 3:14, "And God said unto Moses, I AM THAT

I AM: and he said, Thus shalt thou say unto the children of Israel, I AM hath sent me unto you" (KJV).

The Godhead transcends space. For creation's sake, They have designated a place called heaven as Their headquarters, but They cannot be limited by any spatial considerations. Ponder for a moment the size of Their universe. It would take the *Voyager* spacecraft, traveling at 40,000 miles per hour, 70,000 years to reach the nearest star beyond our sun.[1] So, we are effectively trapped in our little corner of the cosmos.

Light, on the other hand, roars along at 186,000 miles *per second.* That translates into an astonishing 670 million miles per hour.[2] Light can make thirty-one round trips between Los Angeles and New York in the snap of a finger. Even at that off-the-charts speed, it takes two million years for light to get to the nearest galaxy beyond our own.[3] It takes *billions* of years for light to get to the farthest galaxies scientists have spotted through the Hubble telescope.

And where does our universe end? How can it just go on and on and on? And if it does end, what's beyond that? The Trinity transcends even that unlimited concept of space. Because They created the universe, They must be bigger than what They made.

The Godhead transcends the principle of cause/effect on which everything in our world is built. They had no cause, *no beginning.*

They transcend the three dimensions that circumscribe our living. They exist in forms and realms that we cannot understand, which is why They are able to appear and disappear with such ease. "Disappear" simply means that They have moved outside of our three-dimensional awareness.

Any attempt to comprehend the Godhead runs up against these and other amazing attributes that we do not have the mental capacity to compute. We simply don't possess the brain power, the proper synapse connections. God's words through Isaiah capture the theme: " 'For My thoughts are not your thoughts, / Nor are your ways My ways,' says the LORD. / 'For as the heavens are higher than the earth, / So are My ways higher than your ways, / And My thoughts than your thoughts' " (Isaiah 55:8, 9, NKJV).

Thankfully, *the Trinity's transcendence is only half of the story in Scripture.* The Godhead is also what theologians call "immanent," which means They have chosen to make Themselves known to man and draw close to created beings like ourselves. Immanence has to do with God graciously descending to our level to enter into an intimate relationship with us. Immanence is what enables us to call God "Savior" and "Friend."

In order for the church to reflect the fullness of the Trinity, it must emphasize *both* aspects of the Godhead, Their transcendence *and* Their immanence—Their "other-ness" and Their closeness. Without that dual emphasis, the church, and individual Christians, as well, will have a distorted picture of God and be unable to relate to Him in a balanced, healthy way.

If we focus primarily on God's greatness, He can seem hopelessly remote and unknowable. On the other hand, if we focus primarily on His closeness, He can seem too much like us, and we can lose the sense of wonder and awe that makes up the basis of all true worship and humility. That is essentially what happened to Lucifer. He brought God down to his own level. The Scriptures sum up the tragic story:

> "How you are fallen from heaven,
> O Lucifer, son of the morning!
> How you are cut down to the ground,
> You who weakened the nations!
> For you have said in your heart: . . .
> 'I will also sit on the mount of the congregation
> On the farthest sides of the north;
> I will ascend above the heights of the clouds,
> *I will be like the Most High*' "
> (Isaiah 14:12–14, NKJV; italics supplied).

For centuries the Roman Catholic Church focused almost exclusively on transcendence—teaching that God is only knowable by a few chosen insiders in authority. In reaction, Protestants traditionally put much more emphasis on the closeness of the Godhead. Seventh-day Adventists have, for the most part, followed the Protestant tradition and made immanence central to their teaching. But if we are truly called to reveal to the world the multidimensional aspects of the Trinity, we need to give renewed attention to the awesomeness of God, as well.

Recently my wife and I visited our daughter in the Washington, D. C., area. She took us to the National Cathedral for Easter services. We could see the lofty edifice from quite a distance. The 514-foot-long cathedral is the second largest in the United States and took from 1907 to 1990 to complete.[4]

As we neared, it loomed above us in ornate splendor. Upon entering I could feel my heart draw into itself the palpable sense of grandeur. Our eyes were spontaneously drawn upward along the thick granite columns to the lofty vaulted ceiling above.

The long center aisle leads up to a wide, elevated altar resplendent with banners, stone carvings, hand-crafted furniture, and lush floral arrangements. The altar transitions into a large open room beyond, flanked by two sets of carefully wrought wooden benches for the choir. The twenty-six-foot Rose window, which contains 10,500 pieces of stained glass, highlights the interior.[5] A pipe organ fills the immense sanctuary with music that lifts you involuntarily to a higher spiritual plain. Worship comes easily. In that special place the awesome side of God seems so much more accessible.

My daughter told us that when she feels overwhelmed by life or is confronted by some intractable problem, she periodically comes to the National Cathedral to regain perspective, to remember that God is indeed bigger than all of her needs. Such an awareness balances her understanding of Divinity.

It is important that congregations present a balanced view of the Trinity because a lack of attention to Their transcendence can have a very detrimental influence on certain aspects of church life. There are several ways that a diminished emphasis on the awesomeness of God can adversely impact the ability of churches to function well.

Problem 1: Laodicea

According to Scripture, the mantra of Laodicea is, " ' "I am rich, have become wealthy, and have need of nothing" ' " (Revelation 3:17, NKJV). Lack of spiritual humility is the sure result of neglecting the greatness of God. When Isaiah witnessed the extraordinary power of the Almighty, he exclaimed, " 'Woe is me, for I am undone! / Because I am a man of unclean lips, / And I dwell in the midst of a people of unclean lips; / *For my eyes have seen the King, / The LORD of hosts'* " (Isaiah 6:5, NKJV; italics supplied).

John in Revelation describes the experience of the four living creatures that live in close proximity to God's mighty throne: "Day and night they never stop saying: / 'Holy, holy, holy is the Lord God Almighty, who was, and is, and is to come' " (Revelation 4:8, NIV).

The foundation of true humility is understanding who we are, not in relation to other faulty human beings but in relation to God. Even though each of us is of infinite worth, our world is only a microscopic speck in the cosmos. We know only a miniscule portion of the truth about the universe. Our own resources are extremely limited. So, where is there room for spiritual pride or self-sufficiency?

The most potent antidote to the Laodicean condition is to be blown away by the grandeur of God. Some would even say that we should become well acquainted with God's transcendence before we can safely delve into His intimacy.

Problem 2: Loss of mystery

Because we see ourselves as the people of truth, we can feel an overwhelming compulsion to provide simple, concise answers, no matter how complex the religious topic may be. The transcendence of God, however, calls us to embrace complexity and delivers us from the need to wrap up every answer in a neat little package.

Awhile back my wife and I visited a Sabbath School class of about twelve members. Even though we were few in number, the teacher, who sat behind a large wooden desk, had us all arranged in rows. At some point a class member decided to interrupt the teacher's monologue with what I thought was a deep, provocative question.

The teacher responded without a moment's hesitation, "Well, the obvious answer is that . . ." Discussion over. Further questions in subsequent weeks received a similar response. The saddest thing is that the teacher actually thought he was pretty much covering the territory. The teacher had apparently not moved beyond a formulaic religion in which everything can be summed up in a list of key answers, no matter how blatantly inadequate those answers may be. Clearly he had not yet come to grips with the Infinite.

The "Prayer From Kenya" speaks to the issue: *"From the cowardice that dares not face new truth, from the laziness that is contented with half-truth, from the arrogance that thinks it knows all truth, Good Lord, deliver me. Amen."*[6]

My own lack of attention to the transcendence of God became painfully apparent during my struggle with the age-old question, "Why suffering?" How can a God of love who possesses all power allow human beings to experience such immense amounts of injustice and pain?

Earlier in my Christian experience I had a set of stock answers that kept the darkness of the ugly "why suffering?" question largely at bay. Because my Christian experience for so many years made no room for any significant degree of mystery or uncertainty, I felt compelled to pigeon-hole every instance of suffering into a set of prepackaged responses.

But for some reason, during the last several years, the problem of pain forced itself upon my consciousness with what became an overwhelming insistence. If I was honest with myself, what was I going to do with stories like the following?

A truck driver falls asleep at the wheel and smashes into the back of a parked car, killing seven children ages twenty months to fifteen years.[7]

A thirty-three-year-old pastor is electrocuted while performing a baptism, leaving behind a wife and three children.[8]

The bodies of two young children are discovered in shallow graves, riddled with gunshot wounds inflicted two years before by their father.[9]

Bryan Harvey, age forty-nine; his wife, Kathryn Harvey, age thirty-nine; and their daughters Stella, age nine, and Ruby, age four, are discovered in the basement of their burning home, bound in duct tape and beaten, with their throats cut.[10]

Five children, ages nine to sixteen, are killed when lightning strikes a large metal cross where they were praying.[11]

More than eighteen thousand people die from a 7.6 earthquake in Pakistan, India, and Afghanistan. Among the dead are four hundred and fifty children killed when their school buildings collapsed.[12]

Hundreds of thousands die in a tsunami from the Indian ocean.

The tragedies, of course, could be multiplied millions and millions of times throughout the centuries and around the globe. When I allowed myself to dwell more fully on the extent of the horror, the short list of responses to suffering that had preserved my faith for so many years became terribly inadequate. That rudimentary list had four main points:

a. *God wants the victim to learn some spiritual lesson.* God can certainly allow someone to endure suffering in order to help them learn and grow, but this answer is tricky at best. What lesson were the million little kids who were murdered in the Nazi concentration camps supposed to learn?
b. *God is using the person's faith to inspire others.* There are indeed times when people have found inspiration in a sufferer's faith. But there are also many situations in which evil has caused both the victim and/or their loved ones to shake their fist at God and angrily renounce belief forever.
c. *God has to allow these atrocities to take place so that the watching universe can realize the full horror of sin.* May I respectfully respond, "Do we think the watching universe is stupid?" Even I, with my limited perceptions, have seen more than

enough evil in my brief lifetime to know that sin is extremely bad news.

d. *God will bring meaning out of the suffering.* This also can be true. But there are countless instances of suffering where my brain could not imagine there being any meaning or purpose. I could not find in the definitions of the words *meaning* and *purpose* a way to encompass the horrors I was reading about. In my mind it did no good to say, "God will make it clear in the future," because that was simply postponing the inevitable recognition of its utter meaninglessness.

I felt trapped and cornered. My former solutions were useful on a very limited scale, and I had nothing else to grasp on to spiritually. Nowhere else to turn for answers. I felt completely adrift because I hadn't been taught how to relate to such deep perplexity. I labeled my uncertainty as faithlessness and felt my hold on God begin to weaken.

After much spiritual meandering, I have come to realize that my search should not be to try to answer the question, "Why suffering?" That question is clearly inexplicable this side of the kingdom. *What I really needed was to discover how to incorporate the appalling lack of answers into an ongoing trust relationship with God.*

Studying God's transcendence has opened the way. It has given me two concepts that I now hang on to in the face of the monstrous hurt all around us.

The first is that the operations of an infinite God in our sinful world will inevitably involve much mystery. A keen awareness of His transcendence should lead us to expect that His works in our earthly realm will often appear inexplicable. Considering how very different God is from us, it should come as no surprise that His decisions periodically confront us with immense perplexity. Rather than reaching for inadequate stock responses, we would be more God-honoring and life-giving to simply say, "It makes no sense to me." It is OK to admit "I don't have a clue." Pat answers devalue the depth and complexity of another's hurt.

My second conclusion is that because God is so transcendent, He will be able to provide entirely new ways of thinking about meaning and purpose that are far beyond anything I can conceive of now. Up until that point I was trying to limit God to the definitions in *Webster's* dictionary. But the bigger He got and the more unlike me He became, the more accepting I was of the idea that His infinite wisdom has other, greatly expanded ways of conceptualizing meaning and purpose that can, in fact, encompass all the world's pain. Rather than projecting my current understandings into the future as I had before, now I can believe that in heaven our eyes will be opened to remarkable ways of making sense out of apparent senselessness.

I used to think that when Job pleaded in anguish for answers, the Lord's response was pretty callous. But I now see that the Lord was giving Job the best answer possible in the face of such appalling difficulty: "Put your full weight on My transcendence, trust My infinite ways and understanding, and lean on the fact that I am God." The Scriptures record,

> "Where were you when I laid the foundations of the earth?
> Tell Me, if you have understanding. …
> "Have you commanded the morning since your days began,
> And caused the dawn to know its place, …?
> "Have you entered the springs of the sea?
> Or have you walked in search of the depths? …
> "Can you bind the cluster of the Pleiades,
> Or loose the belt of Orion? …
> "Can you lift up your voice to the clouds,
> That an abundance of water may cover you?
> "Can you send out lightnings, that they may go,
> And say to you, 'Here we *are!*'?"
> (Job 38:4, 12, 16, 31, 34, 35, NKJV).

The key to regaining my spiritual health was to learn to embrace the mystery that transcendence brings, to uphold it, and value it as an essential element of our faith. Certainty must live alongside uncertainty. The more complex God becomes in our eyes, the more comfort we can feel in the face of deep ambiguity.

Problem 3: False expectations

For many years I believed that the longer I was a Christian the less uncertainty I should feel. I assumed that as my faith grew, the areas of perplexity in my walk with God would narrow and diminish.

My experience has been just the opposite. The longer I am a Christian, the more perplexities I have had to wrestle with. I have now come to realize that such an experience is, in fact, *quite normal.* The more deeply we appreciate the infiniteness of God, the more we will be challenged by His complexity.

On a beautiful summer day about three months before my sixth birthday, I said to my mother on the way outdoors, "I may be a little late for lunch. I'm going to make a *perpetual motion machine* today." I had heard Mr. Rogers mention the concept on TV. I attributed the fact that no one had ever made one to sheer laziness.

My plan was to fill a bathtub with water until it overflowed then let the stream turn a little paddle wheel that would shoot the water back around into the tub again. Once started, I imagined such a marvel could go on spilling and paddling forever unless halted by human hands.

I planned on using some leftover wooden shingles from a construction site for the paddle and the tub that my friend Johnny Parker used to feed his two horses. As I headed down the street toward the Parker residence, I had the additional brainstorm of letting three or four cod fish live in the water for effect.

When I told Johnny about my plan, he immediately grasped its significance and made the tub available. Filling it went fine, and then the whole thing pretty much went downhill from there. After seven hours of fruitless fiddling, I finally realized that I had forgotten to factor in gravity.

Years later, when I studied physics in high school and learned about vectors, angular momentum, kinetic energy, and diffuse reflection, my parents didn't think I was getting dumber because I raised so many questions. No, they understood that the more you know, the more you realize how much more there is to know.

An experienced astronomer has many more questions and perplexities to grapple with than does a casual observer of the evening sky. A master musician wrestles with issues of interpretation and nuance that never occur to a youngster banging out "Twinkle, Twinkle" on Grandma's upright piano.

So it is in the Christian life. God's transcendence inevitably draws us into ever deepening issues and concepts. Uncertainties in the Christian life often come because we are transitioning from a simple faith to one that has more substance and staying power. The old answers don't fit as they used to. The old understandings don't encompass all that we now see. It takes far more faith to deal with uncertainty than certainty.

I take comfort in the words of Howard Hendricks: "Anyone who thinks he has all the answers is not up to date on the questions."[13]

Problem 4: Exclusivity

Because of a limited understanding of God, we can come to believe that truth is only to be found within Adventism. But when we realize how immensely complex the Godhead is, we can no longer assume that one group, no matter how enlightened, could understand it all. We can be intensely thankful for the great number of special insights and understandings God has given the Seventh-day Adventist Church. Yet, we should also feel an obligation to enter into genuine dialogue with others to discover what aspects of His character and activities God has revealed to them.

As Elizabeth O'Connor has commented, "Dialogue requires a clear, radical, and arduous commitment to listening. Essential to that listening is knowing in the deepest recesses of our being that we really know very little about most things, and that the truth may rest with some unlikely soul."[14]

Problem 5: Little emotion

A denomination that possesses abundant truth must guard against making religion too intellectual. Emotion is a normal and important ally in our spiritual journey.

Few things evoke emotion more readily than being in the presence of grandeur. It is nearly impossible to stand unmoved while watching an intense lightning storm or to remain indifferent when the northern lights transform the night skies into immense, undulating sheets of kaleidoscopic color. Our mouths involuntarily drop open, and a surge of awe courses through our veins. Such events evoke feelings that help offset the numbing influence of our high-tech, impersonal culture. Likewise, inner stirrings evoked by contemplating the transcendent glory of God help balance the downward pull of anxiety and temptation in the Christian life.

Sometimes we're afraid that tapping into religious feelings will turn our brains to mush and cause us to abandon all spiritual reason. But avoiding emotion for fear of excess, walls off a large part of our lives from the Holy Spirit. Nurturing emotion in the Christian life frees us from the shackles of formalism and puts us in touch with an indispensable source of motivation and commitment. It opens us to empathy for others.

Emotion cannot be forced, but it can be cultivated. Churches can intentionally create situations where spiritual feelings are coaxed forward and affirmed. Jesus modeled a wide range of emotions from joy over repentant sinners to despair at being separated from His heavenly Father. He laughed at parties, cried at funerals, and lashed out in anger in the face of excruciating injustice.

I'm trying to let more of my feelings emerge from hibernation. I am almost at the point where I'll let my emotions show through right during the church service. Someday soon I'm going to turn to the person next to me in the pew, point toward heaven, and whisper "Hallelujah."

Summarizing the theme of God's transcendence, Donald Macleod observes, "The truth is that the very first assumption we have to make when we set out to understand God is that we have little, finite minds and that there is no way that he can be made to fit neatly into our words and concepts. A point comes (soon) when we have to stop speaking and writing because words fail us. . . . We have come to the point (arguably the highest point in religious experience) where we glimpse the abyss which revelation has opened up for us and cry with Paul: 'Oh, the depth of the riches of the wisdom and knowledge of God!

How unsearchable are his judgments, and his paths beyond tracing out!'(Romans 11:33)."[15]

Henry Drummond wrote insightfully, " 'A science without mystery is unknown, ... a religion without mystery is absurd.' "[16]

---

1 http://cassfos02.ucsd.edu/public/tutorial/Intro.html, December 7, 2006.

2 http://en.wikipedia.org/wiki/Speed_of_light, December 7, 2006.

3 http://library.thinkquest.org/03oct/01944/light.htm, December 7, 2006.

4 http://www.exploredc.org/index.php?id=179, December 7, 2006.

5 Ibid.

6 "Prayer From Kenya" in Howard G. Hendricks, *Color Outside the Lines* (Nashville, Tenn.: W Publishing Group, 1998), p. 41; italics in original.

7 http://www.cnn.com/2006/LAW/02/03/bus.crash/index.html, December 7, 2006.

8 http://www.cbsnews.com/stories/2005/10/31/national/main995829.shtml, December 7, 2006.

9 http://www.cnn.com/2005/US/12/03/missing.children/index.html, December 7, 2006.

10 http://www.foxnews.com/story/0,2933,208304,00.html, December 7, 2006.

11 http://www.msnbc.msn.com/id/12467604/.

12 http://www.cnn.com/2005/WORLD/asiapcf/10/09/quake.pakistan/index.html.

13 Howard G. Hendricks, *Color Outside the Lines* (Nashville, Tenn.: W Publishing Group, 1998), p. 88.

14 Elizabeth O'Connor, *The New Community* (New York: Harper & Row, 1976), p. 103.

15 Donald Macleod, *Shared Life: The Trinity and the Fellowship of God's People* (Tain, Ross-shire, Scotland: Christian Focus Publications, 1994), p. 52.

16 Quoted in ibid., p. 52.

Chapter 6

Incarnation

When we lived in Maine we owned three acres of semiforested, rural land. We couldn't see our neighbors on one side and could barely see the ones on the other. The distances meant we didn't *have* to talk to them; so, we didn't.

I did manage on one occasion, however, to make a significant contact with one of those neighbors, even though I wouldn't exactly characterize it as witnessing. On a cloudless July day, I was gripped by a spasm of interest in sprucing up our front yard. As I surveyed the situation, it seemed to me that things would look a whole lot better if I could get rid of the branches from the neighbor's property that were hanging over the northern edge of our weed-infested lawn.

A couple of days later I saw the neighbor's son walking down the street and got his permission to go onto their land and "do a little trimming." After lopping off the offending lower branches, I was in a quandary how to reach the ones higher up. What to do? Should I get a ladder? Climb? I was hot, frustrated, and in a hurry; so, I just cut the trees down. The neighbor owned a whole forest anyway. What difference could four or five little oaks make?

That night the neighbor's wife called. "Is this Mr. Johnson?" she asked.

"Yes," I replied.

And the shouting began.

"You're in for some real trouble, mister! First of all, you trespassed on our property! [This was technically incorrect.] Then you destroyed our trees! You had no right! You had *absolutely* no right! None!"

The lady could cram more exclamation-punctuated sentences into one breath than anyone I ever met, including my ill-tempered elementary-school bus driver. When she finally finished scolding, I hurriedly put on my sneakers and rushed down the road to grovel and eat dirt. This sorry episode resulted in some serious pricking of my conscience over the absence of any positive connection with the people around us.

My conscience got twanged pretty hard again about three years ago when I was contacted by a member of a large Seventh-day Adventist church. He asked if I wanted to be considered for an opening on the pastoral staff. I pursued it to the next level, which involved a phone interview with the senior pastor, an associate, and the other members of the search committee.

At the appointed time I called, and the questions started. As things progressed, I felt it was going quite well. Then, about half an hour in, the pastor asked, "How important do you feel it is to share the gospel?"

I considered the question a real softball and confidently replied, "Oh, I think it's very important. I think it's central. Reaching out to others with the good news should be a vital part of every Christian's experience."

Then he nailed me, in a kindly sort of way, "So, what are *you* doing to reach out to those around you?"

Ouch. Fifty volts of embarrassment surged through me. It was like one of those nightmares where you inexplicably wind up running around downtown in your underwear. I paused and then blurted out sheepishly, "I guess I'm not living up to what I preach on that one."

The pastor said he didn't intend to cause me discomfort, but that was a question the staff had agreed to hold each other accountable to. I eventually wound up accepting a different kind of position in Florida instead but was definitely impacted by that exchange.

The Holy Spirit used these situations, and others like them, to plant in me the seeds of a new attitude toward outreach. At the same time, the Spirit was opening my mind more fully to some important theological concepts.

As I studied the Trinity's values and priorities, I was reminded that Their way of reaching people in need is to draw close to them, to identify with them as much as possible, and relate to them in terms they can understand. The pinnacle of that endeavor was, of course, the incarnation of Christ.

Long ago the Trinity's love led Them to make a stunning decision. As a Representative of the Godhead, Christ would leave His heavenly throne, put aside all of His divine powers and prerogatives, condescend far down to our level, and become a man. The universe gasped at the news.

The Savior was to develop in a virgin's womb from a handful of embryonic cells. He would exist in a watery cocoon for nine months, dependent on the nourishment from His mother's umbilical cord. He would pass through the birth canal and emerge bloody, naked, and screaming into an unwelcoming world.

Christ didn't visit Nazareth a few weeks out of the year and then spend the rest of the time back in heaven. He *became one of us.* He lived in the Middle East. He grew up in an out-of-the-way rural village. He became dirt poor, spoke the native language, learned a blue-collar trade, worked for minimum wage, worshiped in a synagogue, ran errands, went to the bathroom in the bushes, sweated profusely, stank, ate with His fingers, burped, passed gas, exchanged stories around dinner, and slept in a one-room house squeezed in among snoring siblings.

The apostle Paul captured well the Savior's incredible condescension when he wrote, "... [Jesus] did not count equality with God a thing to be grasped, but emptied himself, taking the form of a servant, being born in the likeness of men. And being found in human form he humbled himself and became obedient unto death, even death on a cross" (Philippians 2:6–8, RSV).

Christ took the initiative to be with those who were in need. He formed close relationships with them, listened carefully to their hopes and fears, taught them whenever possible, and enveloped them in unconditional love.

The Trinity's method of reaching people has powerful implications for the church. If we are to follow the Godhead's example, our primary means of outreach to the community cannot be asking people to come to our meetings and seminars. Such a "come to us" strategy is not portraying a true picture of God. Meetings have their place, but our core approach should be to draw as close to those we are seeking to reach as Jesus did to the people of His day.

It was the example of Jesus' incarnational ministry that finally got my wife and me to decide to get serious about knowing the people in our neighborhood. After settling into our new home in the Sunshine State, we wondered how to begin but were willing to try.

In the housing development where we live, it's hard not to at least say "Good morning" to the people next door because we all have itsy bitsy yardlets. We've gotten to know our neighbors on the right the best—Terry and Maria. They're both from Iran. She's an artist. He's a restaurant owner. We converse, help each other with projects, and exchange lawn stuff.

Recently Terry and his wife knocked on our door and said, "We want you to come over and eat with us. We've prepared a special meal."

My wife and I had just come back home with take-out from Subway. I was a little annoyed at the lack of notice, but we accepted. This lovely couple has decorated the inside of their house beautifully. Terry showed me the barbecue he built in the screened-in porch and proudly pointed to twenty-five or thirty chunks of skewered meat sizzling atop red-hot coals. He turned them expertly, and my stomach did a few turns, as well. My wife and I haven't eaten meat since college. It's been Vege-Links, Vege-burgers, and tofu for decades.

We sat on a raised platform, which is the custom in Iran. The meal consisted of rice, breads, sauces, and, of course, the meat. My wife and I glanced at each other briefly, shrugged, and then downed some cow.

We laughed and told stories and met their grown-up kids, who happened to be visiting. I think it took us to some kind of next level.

During our contacts, I've been trying hard to resist the nasty, guilt-producing, pushy inner voice that shouts, *Tell them about Jesus* now! *Squeeze the gospel in somewhere in the conversation. At least quote a scripture or two. Leave a tract. Something! They might get into a car crash tomorrow and die and be lost forever unless you tell them. What are you waiting for?*

At present, we're simply trying to learn how to love the people around us and see what the Holy Spirit has in mind.

Janet, a middle-aged single mom, lives diagonally across from us. Three weeks ago she was attempting to put in a new front lawn. Florida has instant lawns using two-foot squares of heavy turf. My wife and I saw her struggling and came over to help. We sweated like pigs but enjoyed it. She told us, "Some of my friends drove by and never stopped to give me a hand. But you came." The following week she brought us a gorgeous orchid.

Isabel, a young nurse, lives next door with her two sisters and a brother. The lawn was becoming a hayfield. I figured their lawnmower must be broken, so I took the liberty of mowing the grass. She thanked me the next morning, which opened an opportunity to chat.

Bob lives a couple of doors down with his wife. We've visited several times. He's a retired trucker and has a heart of gold. Once he starts talking to you, however, your morning is toast. His mouth has no apparent braking mechanism. He firmly believes that foreign conspirators have taken over NASA and that a UFO spied on him in 1985.

Connecting with strangers runs counter to who I've been in the past. My natural inclination is to hibernate, to go about my business, to "live and let live." But God is helping me and changing me. My wife and I are making ourselves available to the Spirit, and we're listening. I can relate to Paul Little, who wrote,

> About once every six months the pressure to witness used to reach explosive heights inside me. Not knowing any better, I would suddenly lunge at someone and spout all my verses with a

> sort of glazed stare in my eye. I honestly didn't expect any response. As soon as my victim indicated a lack of interest, I'd begin to edge away from them with a sigh of relief and the consoling thought, "All that will live godly in Christ Jesus shall suffer persecution" (II Timothy 3:12). ... It really shocked me when I finally realized that I, not the cross, was offending people. My inept, unwittingly rude, even stupid approach to them was responsible for their rejection of me and the gospel message.
>
> But as the Scripture says, he who has friends must be a friend himself (Proverbs 18:24). The art of friendship has been lost by many Christians because they feel their time is being wasted when it's not invested in a specifically religious [discussion]. To be a friend may involve listening to a neighbor's troubles or participating with him in non-religious activities that are of mutual interest socially. It means actively seeking opportunities to show love by running errands, baby-sitting, and performing any other mundane but practical service that will demonstrate the love of Christ. . . .
>
> ... If we are committing our time to the Lord, the Holy Spirit will, in His time, give natural opportunities to speak about the Savior.[1]

The words *evangelism, witnessing,* and *outreach* usually conjure up images of going door to door trying to get annoyed people to sign up for Bible studies. The mere mention of the words makes many Adventists break out in a cold sweat. Those terms have become so loaded down with false meanings that we should give up trying to remodel them. We need a substitute. I think *love* would be a great choice.

If we only understood and trusted God's Grand Canyon–sized vision, we would know that love unleashed can transform the world. It is not a question of whether we should be concerned with information *or* relationships. Both are vital. But the vast majority of people in the United

States, especially the secular minded, won't give a fig how much we know until they know how much we care. It is, in fact, relationships that currently bring the vast majority of people into the church.

"As strange as it may seem to us in the 20th century, the most rapid growth of the church occurred long before the advent of modern media. There was no television, radio, or printed page. First century evangels had just one medium for communicating God's Good News—love."[2]

The Spirit of Prophecy points the way: "Christ's method *alone* will give true success in reaching the people. The Saviour mingled with men as one who desired their good. He showed Hs sympathy for them, ministered to their needs, and won their confidence. *Then* He bade them, 'Follow Me.' "[3]

I have been greatly helped by understanding what I call the Spiritual Interest Line. See the line on the graph below labeled 0 percent at one end and 100 percent at the other. *The line represents a person's level of spiritual interest.*

Spiritual Interest Line

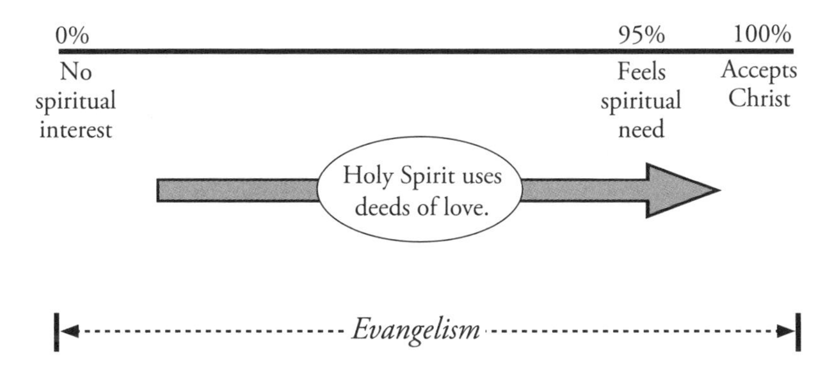

As a person moves along the line from 0 to 95 percent, they are becoming more open to the Spirit but do not yet sense any personal need of God. At 95 percent and above they now become conscious of their spiritual need and want Bible studies. People around us are all at various stages.

It is the patient, loving ministry of Christians that the Holy Spirit uses to move a person from one point on the line to the next. Those ministries simply meet the person's felt need at the time and can take thousands of forms. It could be helping someone start their car, baby-sitting, making dinner for the family while Mom's in the hospital, listening to their troubles, or telling them about your spiritual journey.

Adventists tend to focus to a large extent on working with people who are at 95 to 100 percent. But people don't get to that point overnight, even though it may seem that way. God has used the loving friendship and helping hands of many people over the years, including perhaps Seventh-day Adventists, Baptists, Methodists, Catholics, Pentecostals, and others at different times and different places to bring a person slowly, carefully, step by step, to the point that they eventually reach out for God.

We normally label only the last 5 percent as "evangelism." *But biblically speaking, evangelism means being used by God to help move a person one step further along that line, no matter where that step may be.* We cannot create spiritual interest. We can only discover what the Holy Spirit is already doing and minister to people in whatever way is appropriate at the time.

We would not minister to someone who is at 30 percent in the same way we would to someone who is at 98 percent, and vice versa. We can get a sense of where they are by listening and building trust and do not need to be the entire process.

We could also compare a person's level of spiritual interest to water in a pitcher. If we say that the water spilling out of the spout represents the point when they first feel a need for God, which drop of water was the most important? Obviously all are equally valuable. Likewise, each deed of love is just as important as any other.

I wish I'd understood these concepts when I initially tried to witness to my father. Mom always had a strong faith. Dad was a church-going Methodist during part of my childhood, but then suddenly he stopped attending altogether. He didn't explain why. Over the decades that followed, he never demonstrated any discernible interest in religion.

I am the only Seventh-day Adventist in my family, and after becoming a pastor I longed to share the gospel with my father. Fortunately, my first pastorate placed my wife and me within forty-five minutes' drive of my parents. Dad and I had always been close, so I welcomed the opportunity for us to spend more time together.

Each time I drove to Cape Cod for another visit, my conscience would turn up the guilt. I found myself frequently thinking, *Now how can I turn this conversation around so I can talk to him about Jesus?* The inner pressure to witness grew so great that it eventually became a chore to be around my father. Ironically, the harder I tried to witness, the more ineffective my witness became.

Finally I told God, "I'm going to do my best to demonstrate Your love, and I'm trusting that You'll open opportunities to share whenever possible." For the first time I felt free. I no longer carried the heavy burden of an ulterior motive. I loved my father as fully as I could.

My father spent the last days of his life in a hospital, struggling with congestive heart failure. I visited to offer encouragement and help. He quickly weakened. One day I waited until he and I were alone in the room then I said, "Dad, you know that things are looking pretty serious. I'm not sure how much time is left. I just wanted you to know that I love you and that God loves you very much, as well. God will take care of you and give you peace if you ask. Would you like me to pray for you?" He readily accepted and thanked me earnestly afterward. Before he died, we prayed together several times.

A small thing, perhaps, but I hope it opened a door that in his private moments he chose to walk through.

So much of the goodness that could emerge from Adventist individuals and churches in North America can be stifled by the false notion that projects and endeavors are unworthy unless they are overtly spiritual or lead to baptisms. By imposing such an unbiblical constraint on love, we hinder members from rising up locally and in wider spheres to remedy untold pain and need. Unconditional love with no hidden agendas is God's standard. Ironically, it is that kind of pure love that has the greatest potential, by far, to attract people to the Lord.

Farmers understand that their most important tasks are clearing land, planting seeds, weeding, fertilizing, and watering. If that work is done well, the harvest will naturally come. It is those ministries that should, in fact, receive the vast majority of our resources and attention.

One of the key roles of the local church is to provide the networking and leadership necessary to open up opportunities in the community for members to serve. Many members are longing to plug in and help, but they don't know how or where. That's why they sign on so eagerly for building projects overseas. It gives them a concrete opportunity to love.

Carl Dudley, in his excellent book *Community Ministry,* provides a road map for churches to follow in their attempt to initiate incarnational ministries.[4] His directions include the following steps:

Step 1: *Listen to the community.* How would you feel about going to a doctor who gave you a prescription before he even examined you? It is just as inappropriate to offer a pre-packaged set of programs to the community without first ascertaining the needs.

If we are serious about serving, we must take time to hear what hurts and problems are actually present. That means visiting with a variety of people to do a lot of listening. Members of the church can meet, for example, with the chief of police, mayor, teachers, heads of social agencies, bankers, pastors of other faiths, government officials, business leaders, shopkeepers, factory workers, store clerks, homemakers, teenagers, etc. The members can also seek out the "invisible" people among the poor, handicapped, and elderly. Ellen White counseled, "We should seek to understand the needs of the poor and distressed, and to give them the help that will benefit them most."[5]

Step 2: *Find your church's calling.* You want to find a good match between the church's resources and the community's needs. What are the characteristics of your congregation? What spiritual gifts are present? What has the Spirit equipped your congregation to do? Through prayer and feedback from the members, church leadership can discern which needs God is calling them to meet.

Step 3: *Discover what God is already doing.* Once you determine your direction, find out what God is already doing in the community to meet those needs. You may be initiators of a new ministry. You also may need to come alongside others already engaged in a ministry.

There are many genuine, dedicated Christians in non-Adventist churches. We don't need to adopt their doctrines, but we certainly can join hearts to meet the needs of hurting people all around us. How will these other churches ever learn about Seventh-day Adventists anyway, if we choose to remain apart? The important thing is not what recognition we receive but what is best for the people we are called to serve.

The three steps mentioned above are an ongoing process and not a one-time event.

One of the most well-known and effective incarnational ministries in the U.S. is the Church of Our Savior's outreach to the poor in Washington, D.C. Elizabeth O'Connor, one of the early members of the church, observes, "As we came to see more clearly the faces of those submerged in the crushing poverty of our own city, it became obvious that only those engaged in the struggles of the poor were going to be able to speak to them any message of God's reign."[6]

At one point the members of the church scraped together enough funds to purchase two old, badly run-down tenement buildings and took on the incredibly daunting task of remodeling them for the poor. O'Connor recounts a portion of their experience.

> The members of Jubilee Housing had no less a mission in mind than to put an end to poverty in the city, to secure decent housing for every person at a cost that each could afford, "to proclaim the year of the Lord's favor." …
>
> … On the first of November 1973, the two apartment buildings became the property of Jubilee Housing, Incorporated. Two days later the District of Columbia served the new owners with a three-page list of 900 violations of the housing code.
>
> Gordon Cosby asked his congregation to devote some of the time usually given to preparing for Christmas to help with the

> renovation of the apartments. All kinds of people responded. . . . There was a place for everyone's gift to be used. . . .
>
> To some of us it seemed that we had stumbled on the appropriate way to celebrate the Christmas season. We gave each other gifts of paint rollers, overalls, and books with useful titles, like *The Boiler Room: Questions and Answers.*[7]

An inspiring example of a Seventh-day Adventist church committed to pursuing incarnational ministries is the Miracle Temple in Baltimore, Maryland. The church's motto is, "A local church with a global impact." The members have established various ministries that directly relate to the hurts and needs that people in the inner city struggle with every day. Those ministries emerge from the church's ongoing dialogue with the community.

Their Faith Center is a nonprofit counseling group staffed by professional psychologists and social workers from their own congregation. The Center's board is composed not only of church members but also outside community leaders who share a passion for healing.

Once a month, on Street Ministry Sabbath, church members go to several areas of Baltimore to do programs right on the streets that build friendships and convey the gospel in various ways, including drama-team skits. Prayer warriors go to businesses to pray with the owners and managers. Kids' Night has a variety of activities for local children.

The fourth Sabbath of every month is Community Service Sabbath, when the youth of Miracle Temple team up with other young people in Baltimore to enter the community in full force. The teens serve by doing everything from feeding the homeless to giving aid to individuals displaced by tragedy.

Other types of need-based ministries are initiated and coordinated by Baltimore Adventist Community Services, which is the hub for several Adventist churches in the area, including Miracle Temple. The Community Services center offers traditional clothing and food distribution but also makes a concerted effort to creatively expand into other areas of outreach such as youth training initiatives, job training, and programs to assist families of those who have been incarcerated.[8]

As Adventists we are called to be the most loving people on the planet, and our churches in the United States can touch their local communities with the love of God in a thousand different creative ways.

Pain on a more global scale also cries out for our involvement. For example, with *210,000 children throughout the world dying needlessly every week,*[9] our churches in America can be in the forefront of raising an outcry, urging, lobbying, writing, marching, finding funds, doing whatever it takes. I can't help thinking, *How would I react if one of the children in need was my child?* Christlike love can thrust us into the forefront of tackling AIDS, racial injustice, the slaughter in different parts of Africa, illiteracy, and other major ills in society. This is not a social gospel; it is what love compels us to do in the face of appalling need. It is what gives spiritual utterances credibility.

In the words of Jesus, " 'The Spirit of the Lord is on me, because he has anointed me to preach good news to the poor. He has sent me to proclaim freedom for the prisoners and recovery of sight for the blind, to release the oppressed, to proclaim the year of the Lord's favor' " (Luke 4:18, NIV).

It seems appropriate to close with a quote from Bono, leader of the band U2, when he spoke at a presidential prayer breakfast. "God is in the slums, in the cardboard boxes where the poor play house. God is in the silence of a mother who has infected her child with a virus that will end both their lives. God is in the cries heard under the rubble of war. God is in the debris of wasted opportunity and lives, and God is with us if we are with them. If you remove the yoke from your midst, the pointing of the finger and speaking wickedness, and if you give yourself to the hungry and satisfy the desire of the afflicted, then your light will rise in darkness and your gloom will become like midday and the Lord will continually guide you and satisfy your desire in scorched places."[10]

---

1 Paul Little, *How to Give Away Your Faith* (Westmont, Ill.: InterVarsity Press, 1988), pp. 30, 32.

2 Win Arn, Carroll Nyquist, and Charles Arn, *Who Cares About Love* (Monrovia, Calif.: Church Growth Press, 1986), p. 114.

3 Ellen G. White, *The Ministry of Healing,* p. 143 (italics supplied).

4 Adapted from Carl S. Dudley, *Community Ministry* (Bethesda, Md.: Alban Institute, 2002).

5 Ellen G. White, *The Ministry of Healing,* p. 195.

6 Elizabeth O'Connor, *The New Community*, p. 27.

7 Ibid., pp. 29, 31.

8 See http://www.miracletemple.net and http://www.abetterbaltimore.org.

9 Jane Lampman, "A priority for U.S. churches: Africa's poor," *Christian Science Monitor*, June 19, 2005, quoted from http://www.sojo.net/index.cfm?action=news.display_article&mode=S&NewsID=4872, Dec. 11, 2006.

10 *Sojourners*, February 3, 2006, http://www.sojo.net.

Chapter 7

Community

In the mid-1990s I decided to start a school for pastors in our conference. It didn't make sense at all on paper. I was the associate treasurer, and my pastoral experience was a distant memory. But I had a big dream. I lobbied the powers that be, somehow got a green light, and forged ahead. Pastors would come to the conference office on a volunteer basis one day a month from 9:00 A.M. to 5:00 P.M.

I named the school AsPIRE, which stood for "Assisting Pastors In Reaching Excellence." I was surprised to see fifteen ministers show up at our first meeting, three-quarters of the conference's pastoral staff. I had already been dialoguing with many of them informally for months about God's vision for His church, and they apparently saw this as an opportunity to focus on that vital topic more consistently. Their attendance had far more to do with the depth of their interest than any expertise in me.

Before opening prayer, I asked if there were any needs they wanted mentioned. Without any hesitation, the pastors immediately launched into a lengthy discussion about various professional challenges they were facing. As the minutes ticked by, I found myself getting a little annoyed, because I had planned to cover a lot of material.

The same thing happened at the next three meetings. The sharing before prayer actually grew longer and became even more intense. I could see the earnestness in their eyes and sensed the frustration and concern in their voices. The agenda got short-changed even more.

Eventually it dawned on me, in my incessantly task-driven head, that what was happening at prayer time was that we were being church. Church is primarily about becoming a loving community where people can find help and wholeness. *How ironic,* I thought. *Here I am getting all hot and bothered because the reality of church is intruding on the time I had set aside to read about it!*

At that point I revamped the whole schedule and allotted two full hours at each meeting, first thing in the morning, for sharing experiences and needs. Over time, as the trust level grew, the sharing became more personal in nature. I remember one young pastor telling the group, "Last night my head elder blasted me on the phone for the umpteenth time about nothing. Nothing! I'm sick and tired of his attacks!" Tears welled up in his eyes and his voice quivered. "This isn't what I bargained for. Not at all. I probably shouldn't say this, but I'm very discouraged right now. *Very* discouraged. To tell you the truth, I really feel like giving up." He hung his head in silence.

A pastor from across the room spontaneously got up, walked over, bent down, and gave him a long hug. Other pastors quickly came and knelt beside him. Nothing was said, but I could hear the young man's muffled sobs. He buried his head in his hands. Someone began to sing softly, "What a Friend we have in Jesus." Everyone joined. "All our sins and griefs to bear." Another hymn was sung, lifting the dark clouds with gentle, soothing harmonies.

Someone read a couple of verses from Paul's epistles and then the Psalms. Prayers were offered, deeply moving prayers, full of empathy. Everyone eventually returned to their seats, and then the testimonies began from others who were also experiencing various types of personal pain and perplexity. These religious professionals, who usually feel that they need to look like they have it all together with God, shared as if they had finally found a safe place to be open and honest and unload heavy burdens. One after another they told their story. I sat there in amazement. As I listened, tears welled up in my own eyes.

The sharing time became a remarkable source of caring and hope. Nothing was forced. No one *had* to participate. No one was made to feel uncomfortable. But these pastors had discovered something they obviously valued.

At some point, one of the ministers made a remark I will never forget: "*Now* I can lead my congregation into becoming a true biblical community because, for the first time ever, I've experienced it right here *myself*." We were building something that transcended our own individual needs, a closeness that reflected the very life of God.

Since that time more than ten years ago, I have longed to comprehend more fully and experience more deeply God's purpose for the church, in particular the Seventh-day Adventist Church. One thing I now know more than ever is that being a nurturing, life-giving community of believers is at the very heart of the Godhead's plan.

". . . The fact that we bear the divine image means that we are *made for fellowship*. This is probably the most important point of all. As bearers of God's image, we are made for 'with-ness'. . . . There is a social life in the Godhead itself. The Father, the Son and the Holy Spirit live in community and fellowship. The same must be true of us."[1]

Larry Crabb adds, "Christianity is about the life of the Trinity released in human community."[2] Experiencing togetherness should define church as much as it defines the Trinity.

I frankly was startled to discover that biblically we are to represent God, not primarily as individuals but as the local church, as a whole. It is the life we create together with fellow members that portrays the image of God to nonbelievers. ". . . The primary issue is not the private holiness of the individual Christian. The point is that an entire people give witness to God's plan for the world. . . . The world can be changed only when the people of God itself changes."[3]

Simply because one hundred people are excellent musicians individually does not mean they are an orchestra. In order to play great music, they must put aside their own agendas and commit to playing together, reading off the same page, blending, listening to one another, encouraging one another, and accepting direction. The great symphonies will remain unplayed unless the many become one. We are God's orchestra.

The apostle Paul uses the phrase "one another" in various ways to try to capture some key characteristics of Christian community.

"Be *devoted* to one another in brotherly love" (Romans 12:10, NASB; italics supplied).

"*Honor* one another above yourselves" (Romans 12:10, NIV; italics supplied).

"*Accept* one another . . . just as Christ accepted you, in order to bring praise to God" (Romans 15:7, NIV; italics supplied).

"You seem to me to be well-motivated and well-instructed, quite capable of *guiding and advising* one another" (Romans 15:14, *The Message;* italics supplied).

"You, my brothers, were called to be free. But do not use your freedom to indulge the sinful nature; rather, *serve one another in love*" (Galatians 5:13, NIV; italics supplied).

"*Bear one another's burdens,* and thus fulfill the law of Christ" (Galatians 6:2, NASB; italics supplied).

"*Submit* to one another out of reverence for Christ" (Ephesians 5:21, NIV; italics supplied).

"Therefore *encourage* one another and build each other up" (1 Thessalonians 5:11, NIV; italics supplied).

Paul Sampley sums up the theme of these verses and others like them: "Community is the nurturing context within which the individual is expected to live. There the individual is encouraged to grow, is edified by the love of others, is shored up in weakness, is consoled upon straying, and is called to account when behaving inappropriately. . . .

"The life of faith, the life in Christ, must be lived in the context and care of others. By God's grace, believers are given to one another and for one another. . . .

"For Paul the life of faith cannot be imagined apart from community."[4]

The Bible's emphasis on building Trinity-like communities did not come as entirely good news for me, because I tend to be a very private person. I'm a big-time introvert and can be very happy spending my evenings behind a computer or reading a book. But I have asked Jesus to be Lord of my life, and I want what is important to Him to be important to me. My preference for independence is born of sin and needs to be crucified. I cannot simply say, "It's not my thing" or "I don't feel comfortable doing that" or "I don't have time." We were created for community, and sin has made us think we can make it on our own.

The apostle Peter became a spiritual rock because of the three and a half years he spent interacting with Jesus and the other disciples. John, the hot-headed, power-grabbing Son of Thunder became the apostle of love by being immersed in a Jesus-led community. Simon the Roman-hater even grew to love Matthew the Roman collaborator. Those years of learning how to love were the primary preparation for Pentecost—not just ten days in the upper room. Jesus accomplished His purpose so fully that after His ascension, similar Trinity-like communities developed rapidly from Jerusalem to Rome.

I cannot grow and mature as one of Christ's disciples without entering into community any more than the disciples could. It is not possible to learn in isolation how to love others and ourselves.

John Powell makes this profound observation: "What I am at any given moment in the process of my becoming a person, will be determined by my relationships with those who love me or refuse to love me, with those I love or refuse to love."[5]

One of the most famous fairy tales of all time is that of Rapunzel. In the story, a young lady is imprisoned in a tower by an old witch. Even though the young girl is strikingly beautiful, the witch repeatedly tells her she is ugly in order to keep her from leaving.

One day Rapunzel gazes out the window and sees Prince Charming standing at the base of the tower. She tosses her long golden tresses out of the tower window, and the prince uses her hair as a ladder to climb up and rescue her.

It was not really the tower that kept Rapunzel imprisoned at all; it was the witch's insistence that she was unattractive. When she sees in the eyes of her lover that she is indeed beautiful, she is freed.[6]

That is the gift we can bestow on others, to mirror in our eyes the love of God that makes each person feel beautiful within.

Henri Nouwen, a religion professor, taught at the universities of Notre Dame, Yale, and Harvard. He left teaching to share his life with mentally handicapped people at the L'Arche community of Daybreak in Toronto, Canada. He writes,

> There is one of my friends there who is quite handicapped but a wonderful, wonderful lady. She said to me, "Henri, can you bless me? I want to be blessed." I kept thinking, "What does she mean?"
>
> Janet put her head against my chest and I spontaneously put my arms around her, held her, and [then] looked right into her eyes and said, "Blessed are you, Janet. You know how much we love you. You know how important you are. You know what a good woman you are."
>
> She looked at me and said, "Yes, yes, yes, I know." I suddenly saw all sorts of energy coming back to her. She seemed to be relieved from the feeling of depression because suddenly she realized again that she was blessed. She went back to her place and immediately other people said, "I want that kind of blessing, too."
>
> The people kept walking up to me and I suddenly found myself embracing people. I remember that after that, one of the people in our community who assists the handicapped, a strong guy, a football player, said, "Henri, can I have a blessing, too?" I remember our standing there in front of each other and I

> said, "John," and I put my hand on his shoulder, "you are blessed. You are a good person. God loves you. We love you. You are important."[7]

That is the crucial affirmation we can give each other in God's community.

Terry Wardle reminds us, "Our society is filled with people who have suffered deep emotional woundings. The list of injuries that have occurred to people during childhood alone is almost endless. Physical, emotional and sexual abuse; rejection, shaming, manipulation, abandonment; control, motivation by fear, the absence of all positive affirmations. This is only the tip of what is hidden deep within so many, many people of all ages, genders, and classes.

"But rather than address the wounds head-on, we are taught to hide, stuff, cope, pretend and, if possible, forget them all together."[8]

It is the truth about God's love, forgiveness, and acceptance that can free people, but how can that be comprehended and believed unless it is first witnessed within a loving, nurturing community?[9]

Larry Crabb writes, "I have come to believe that the root of all our personal and emotional difficulties is a lack of togetherness. . . . Tears without an audience, without someone to hear and care, leave the wounds unhealed. When someone listens to our groanings and stays there, we feel something change inside us. Despair seems less necessary; hope begins to stir where before there was only pain."[10]

Community-building is the Trinity's most powerful vehicle for changing lives. It begins with the family unit, moves into the congregation, and expands out from there.

Church members need to interact on many levels and in a variety of ways. But the most promising vehicle for developing in-depth relationships within the body of Christ that I know of is through participation in a small group where ten to twelve people meet regularly to grow together in Christ. It would be wonderful if churches could be filled with such groups. My wife and I have joined several groups in the past. If church is primarily about relationships, then the small-group setting is where those relationships can be developed best.

It appears that many Adventists feel that attendance at the worship service on Sabbath morning is essential but participation in a small group is optional. I believe in attending Sabbath morning services, but if I *had* to choose between that and my small group, the small group would come first every time. Why? Because that is where I can help fulfill the relational mission of Jesus best. It is not far-fetched to say that, in many ways, church is intended to function something like Alcoholics Anonymous. Small groups provide invaluable support, as well as life-giving opportunities to minister to others.

Bill and Nancy had been married for several years. After starting out well, their relationship had, sadly, been heading downhill for some time and was now in serious trouble. It finally deteriorated to the point where Bill told his wife he wanted a divorce.

Prior to this they had been part of a small group for about a year that met for friendship and encouragement. For several months the group had been reading books and watching videos on how to stay in love. The discussions grew more in-depth, and the participants eventually felt comfortable sharing their journey and receiving guidance and suggestions from the others.

All during that time, Bill had been afraid to share his true feelings, even with his wife. When he did give the shocking news, Nancy immediately called some of the group members in great distress. Within minutes, one of the couples hurried to their home. The wife consoled Nancy and the husband asked Bill to go for a walk. As he and Bill circled the neighborhood, the husband listened carefully, offered additional perspectives, and pledged to stand with the hurting couple for support as long as it took to put things back on track.

This loving commitment brought Bill to tears, and by the end of the second lap he could feel a ray of hope awaken within him. He would give the marriage another try, knowing that he and his wife had the assistance of the other couples, no matter what.

Bill and Nancy kept attending group meetings, and the members rallied around them, actually refusing to let them get a divorce. Many nights they sat with them late into the evening, listening, comforting, and offering feedback.

Because of the group's consistent encouragement and love, Bill and Nancy chose to work hard to repair their damaged relationship. Today there has been a complete turnaround. Their marriage has been rescued and placed on a much firmer foundation.[11] Left to themselves, however, their marriage certainly would have died.

Many pastors I talk with wonder why it is so hard to build close relationships among their members. They are especially concerned with why it is so difficult to get wide, ongoing involvement in small groups. Often a handful of groups start up and then, rather than expanding, within a year they fade away. Why doesn't such a ministry thrive? Let me offer a few suggestions.

1. Individualism. Individualism is epidemic in North America. C. Norman Kraus observes, "In contemporary American society, it is an unquestioned assumption that the individual takes precedence over the group. 'Freedom' is defined as individual independence."[12] Our country was birthed by the Declaration of Independence. People's everyday conversations are permeated with talk of individual "rights."

We are a consumer society, both materially and relationally. If a person doesn't get out of a marriage what they expected, they file for divorce. Many are afraid of commitment because it might hinder their ability to do as they please. As Charles Reich has ominously stated, *"America is one vast, terrifying anti-community."*[13]

The disease of individualism can easily infect church life, as well. We even sing a song that says, "Dare to be a Daniel, dare to stand *alone.*" The ideal end-time Adventist is often viewed as someone who is able to survive by depending on God alone.

One of the best antidotes for individualism is to help people rediscover God's wonderful plan for the church in a small-group setting, where they not only study about church in Scripture but also experience it relationally, as well. Learning about "church" is like learning about love. We can't understand love simply by reading about it. Not until we experience love and give it can we begin to comprehend its true meaning. So it is with church. We need to learn not just cognitively but relationally, as well; not just with the head but also with the heart. Participating in a small group that lives out God's vision among the participants can open up an entirely new perspective and value system.

Small groups will ultimately die, however, if they are seen as simply another vehicle for getting individual needs met. Meeting group members' needs is important, but our highest calling, our ultimate goal, must be to build a life together that reflects the love within the Godhead and spills over to bless others. It is God's agenda that gets top priority, not mine. It is the revelation of Himself to the world that needs to be uppermost.

The whole process of becoming an Adventist can, inadvertently, breed spiritual individualism. The usual perception seems to be that if a convert accepts Christ as Savior and adheres to our doctrines, that person is prepared for membership. They are then voted into a church in moments and don't even have to be present. But nowhere in the process have they been asked to commit themselves to a radical relational reorientation, to making community-building central to their lives. Nowhere have they been "transculturized."

They can attend church for years without feeling any need to connect with others on a deep enough level to represent the image of God. Very few seem to realize that when they were baptized "in the name of the Father, and of the Son, and of the Holy Spirit" they were making a public commitment to Trinitarian living. (See Matthew 28:19.) A person's commitment to God's vision for the church is just as important as their commitment to Sabbath or any other doctrine.

It would be far better if the primary goal of evangelism was to involve people in biblical community first and then teach them about our beliefs.[14] Once they have learned to value *both* belonging and believing, they can then be brought into church membership.

2. Isolation. Another impediment to building true biblical community is the terrible isolation that is so characteristic of today's society.

Seventy-three-year-old Adele Gaboury had helpful neighbors. They mowed her lawn for free and did whatever else seemed to need doing around her yard. The only thing they didn't do was to check if she was alive. On a Monday, police broke into her little blue house and found Adele's skeletal remains where they had apparently lain for what was later estimated to be up to four years. " 'It's not really a very friendly neighborhood,' " said Eileen Dugan, seventy, who lived just twenty feet away.[15]

Isolation has become the norm in America. Dinner is too often a disjointed affair, with everyone eating separately. Video games, TVs, and computers mean we can happily entertain ourselves. Because news broadcasts consistently focus on the worst people in town, we worry that our neighbors might be crooks or child molesters and become even more isolated. The convenience of the Internet lets us do our banking and shopping without coming in contact with human beings. If we need cash, we can go to the ATM and avoid talking to anyone. Our schedules are so hectic we have little time to interact on a meaningful level, even with our own family.

The problem is that true community cannot become a reality if it is squeezed in among everything else we are already doing. Even a weekly small group is not enough to build true oneness if it is not reinforced by other interactions among the participants. True community will remain elusive if we don't take inventory, reassess our priorities, and restructure our lives to allow much more time to connect at various levels with family, fellow believers, and others.

Luke tells us that early Christians "devoted themselves to the apostles' teaching *and to the fellowship, to the breaking of bread* [eating together] and to prayer" (Acts 2:42, NIV; italics supplied).

3. Misunderstanding the purpose of our doctrines. If biblical truth becomes an end in itself, building in-depth relationships will be seen as helpful but not essential. It is only when we come to realize the doctrines were given to make us more loving that community-building is given its rightful place.

4. Urgency. "The problem has been that preoccupation with future reality has undercut present expectation and possibility."[16] Our emphasis on the nearness of the second coming of Christ can make us feel that we don't have time to invest in the slow, gradual business of community-building. If we see our primary role as only that of a spiritual Paul Revere, then we'll give first importance to passing on the warning and getting ourselves ready. If we believe the forest is about to burn down, why spend time planting oak trees?

When I was a junior theology major in 1970, I thought the return of the Lord was so near that I decided to skip my senior year of college. I told my fiancée that we would buy an old bus, travel the country preaching, and live off freewill offerings. Someone eventually talked me out of that headstrong adventure, and I went on to graduate. But the urgency of the Second Coming still dominated my thinking.

Then H. M. S. Richards Sr. died. And then H. M. S. Richards Jr. died. No two people expected Christ to return in their lifetime more than they did. I began wrestling with the fact that the signs in nature we usually use to indicate the nearness of Christ's return, such as the earthquake of 1755 and the Dark Day of 1780, occurred a very, very long time ago.

I am now within shouting distance of sixty and what seemed utterly impossible in my early twenties—dying before Christ returns—seems like a very real possibility today. I still certainly believe that Jesus could come at any time, but the passage of so many years has led me to step back and take a broader, more in-depth look at God's plan for His people. It was in that search that I discovered how woeful my understanding of the Trinity's purpose for the church really was.

I don't have any word from Scripture on when the Second Coming will be. I do, however, see very clear instruction in the Bible on what the church is supposed to be doing in the meantime. I have decided to pour my life into recapturing our fundamental purpose and will leave the timing of the Second Coming up to God. I also realize now that becoming a biblical community as God intended is the best thing we can do to prepare people for the Second Coming anyway. It fits perfectly with Jesus' mandate to grow disciples within nurturing congregations (see Matt. 28:18–20).

The Spirit of Prophecy clearly reveals God's priorities: "Enfeebled and defective as it may appear, the church is the one object upon which God bestows in a special sense His supreme regard. It is the theater of His grace, in which He delights to reveal His power to transform hearts."[17]

Pastor Randy Frazee has a son who was born without a left hand. One day, the little boy's Sunday School teacher was talking to the children about church. To illustrate her point, she folded her hands together as if praying then turned them inside out, wiggled her fingers, and said, "Here's the church, here's the steeple, open the door and see all the people."

She asked the class to do it, without thinking about the pastor's son. In a moment the boy next to him, a friend since infancy, reached out his own left hand and said, "Let's do it together." The two joined their hands and made the church, the steeple, and all ten people.

That is the essence of biblical community.

"God has one priority project throughout history, one that he will bring to climactic completion at the end of history—the formation of the new community."[18]

---

1 Donald Macleod, *Shared Life: The Trinity and the Fellowship of God's People,* p. 61; italics in original.

2 Larry Crabb, *Connecting* (Nashville, Tenn.: Word Publishing, 1997), p. 95.

3 Gerhard Lohfink, *Jesus and Community* (Philadelphia: Fortress Press, 1982), pp. 131, 138.

4 J. Paul Sampley, *Walking Between the Times* (Minneapolis: Fortress Press, 1991), p. 43.

5 Julie A Gorman, *Community That Is Christian* (Wheaton, Ill.: Victor Books, 1993), p. 105.

6 John Powell, *Why Am I Afraid to Love* (Niles, Ill.: Argus Communication, 1972), pp. 48, 49.

7 Message by Henri Nouwen, "Solitude, Community and Ministry" Pro-

gram #3706, First air date Nov. 7, 1993, http://www.30goodminutes.org/csec/sermon/nouwen_3706.htm

8 Terry Wardle, *Wounded: How You Can Find Inner Wholeness and Healing in Him* (Camp Hill, Penn.: Christian Publications, 1994), p. 19.

9 See Terry Wardle, pp. 74, 75; Tod E. Bolsinger, *It Takes a Church to Raise a Christian* (Grand Rapids, Mich.: Brazos Press, 2004), p. 169; C. Norman Kraus, *The Authentic Witness* (Grand Rapids, Mich.: Eerdmans, 1979), p. 166.

10 Larry Crabb, *Connecting,* pp. 32, 127.

11 Adapted from Gary Smalley, *Making Love Last Forever* (Dallas: Word Publishing, 1996), pp. 206–209.

12 C. Norman Kraus, *The Authentic Witness* (Grand Rapids, Mich.: Eerdmans, 1979), p. 76.

13 Julie A Gorman, *Community That Is Christian*, p. 78; italics in original.

14 Richard Rice, *Believing, Behaving, Belonging* (Roseville, Calif.: Association of Adventist Forums, 2002), p. 121.

15 Randy Frazee, *The Connecting Church* (Grand Rapids, Mich.: Zondervan, 2001), p. 109.

16 C. Norman Kraus, *The Community of the Spirit* (Scottdale, Penn.: Herald Press, 1993), p. 14.

17 Ellen G. White, *The Acts of the Apostles,* p. 12.

18 Gilbert Bilezikian, *Community 101,* p. 43.

Chapter 8

Oneness

Camping is right up there with mowing grass and moving on my list of unpleasant things to do. Don't get me wrong, campfires and marshmallow roasts are fine. Even a mosquito carcass in the rice and beans can be overlooked. It's the camping Neanderthals I can't abide. I actually seem to attract them. A campground might be empty when I check in, but I will invariably select a site right next to the one that will later be occupied by the loudest, most obnoxious drunken people ever to spend a night under the stars. It has happened too many times to be mere chance. It is as if I am in the grip of some sadistic cosmic fate. It is always a different group, but these brutes invariably

- ooze testosterone;
- sport eighty to one hundred weird tattoos;
- wear undersized, grease-stained T-shirts that say "Genius at work";
- haul a ten-foot trailer filled with cheap beer;
- have five hundred loudspeakers installed in their monster truck;
- arrive after 1:00 A.M. and party till sunrise;
- are shocked they're not the only ones camping there;
- don't have a clue how to put up a tent.

I used to sit in my own tent and fume all night. But on some camping trip somewhere, I cracked. I simply couldn't take it anymore. With my wife clutching at my pinstriped pajamas and whispering in a muffled scream, "Are you cra-a-a-z-zy! Don't go out there! They'll kill you!" I opened the tent flap around 2:00 A.M. and stomped over to my tormentors. I was like a man possessed. Years of pent-up fury came spewing out in an uncontrollable rage.

I spoke firmly, "Don't you think you fellows are being a bit noisy?" They turned on me with swearing, offensive references to my beloved mother, and threats of bodily harm. Outnumbered eight to one, I chose life and ran.

On the next camping trip, I changed my tactics. Instead of confronting the group myself, I walked in the moonlight to the ranger's log home at the edge of the campground. I banged on his door until he appeared, bleary-eyed and yawning.

"Do you have any idea what's happening right now out there in your camp?" I said, pointing back in the general direction of the infraction. I explained briefly. He listened intently, turned back into the house, emerged five minutes later in full ranger uniform, jumped into his truck, and sped away in a cloud of dust. I ran to catch up.

As I neared the Neanderthals, I could hear the tall, burly ranger conclude his incensed lecture by shouting, "I want all of you out of here in ten minutes. And if I hear so much as a burp from any of you while you're packing, I'll have you all arrested!" I can't begin to tell you how immensely satisfying that speech was for me.

The words of Jesus, " 'Foxes have holes and birds of the air have nests, but the Son of Man has no place to lay his head,' " indicate that He spent many nights camping with the disciples amidst cold, bugs, wild animals, and perhaps a few first-century Neanderthals (Matthew 8:20, NIV).

Evening after evening, Christ and His followers would gather around a little fire and talk, exchange stories, reflect on the day, sing, and laugh a lot. Spending enormous amounts of quality time at these campouts was a major element in the training of the Twelve. He also taught them during the many miles they walked from one town to the next.[1] For most of three decades, the Savior had built furniture and houses. Now He was building people, constructing the foundation of the Christian church.

The Lord's deepest heart-longing for this motley group of men is best expressed in His vitally important prayer in John 17. In this final petition prior to Gethsemane, Jesus sums up the central purpose of His entire ministry for the Twelve. He pinpoints exactly why He has invested so much of Himself in them. Four times within that brief prayer He emphasizes the same point, not only because it weighed heavily on His heart but also because He didn't want it to be missed:

" '... that they may be one . . .' " (verse 11, NKJV)
" 'that they all may be one . . .' " (verse 21, NKJV)
" '... that they also may be one . . .' " (verse 21, NKJV)
" '... that they may be made perfect in one . . .' " (verse 23, NKJV)

There can be no doubt that creating oneness among His followers was the all-consuming passion of Jesus' heart.

And the Savior left no doubt, as well, about the quality of oneness He has in mind for the church. Remarkably, He wants His followers to manifest the same kind of closeness that exists within the Trinity itself!

" '... even as We are one' " (verse 11, RSV)
" '... as You, Father, are in Me, and I in You' " (verse 21, NKJV)
" '... just as We are one' " (verse 22, NKJV)

Living in unity with the Father and the Holy Spirit was all that Jesus had ever known, not only since His birth but for an unlimited eternity of years before that. The oneness within the Godhead is so profound that it wasn't until late in the fourth century A.D. that the church finally figured out a way to describe it.

After much study and discussion, the religious leaders of the fourth century concluded that the Members of the Godhead all shared what they called *homoousios*. "It is a transliteration of a compound Greek word containing the prefix *homo,* which means 'the same,' and the verb *ousios,* which means . . . 'essence of being,' " or nature.[2] We do not worship three Gods who have a very close relationship; we worship *one God, made up of Three divine Persons, who are one in nature, character, and purpose.*[3]

Oneness is so vital to the Godhead that the only way Jesus could minister as He walked this earth was to frequently spend entire nights in prayer communing with the Others. When Christ became separated from the Father in Gethsemane, and again on the cross, He was so adversely impacted that He sweat blood, screamed in agony, and died. He could not survive the loss of that essential union. *And in His John 17 prayer, Jesus uses that incredible bond within the Godhead as a model for relationships within the church.*

In order to provide us with a concrete example of what Trinitylike oneness would look like among human beings, Jesus gave top priority to creating that oneness among the disciples. From power-hungry James and John to head-strong Peter, the Twelve were a volatile, arrogant, self-centered, thick-headed, highly opinionated mixture of men. But the Scriptures tell us that after Jesus' ascension they were of "one accord," and "of one heart and one soul" (Acts 2:46; 4:32, NKJV). Through unparalleled leadership and love, Jesus managed, in just three years, to create within these faulty followers a miracle of jaw-dropping unity.

In His prayer, Christ makes it clear that manifesting such unity should be at the core of the church's mission strategy. During His petition, Jesus speaks to His Father and asks that His followers be one so that " '*the world may believe* that You sent Me' " (John 17: 21, NKJV; italics supplied) and " '*the world may know* that You have sent Me, and have loved them as You have loved Me' " (verse 23, NKJV; italics supplied).

The Lord's desire was that the oneness among the disciples, and His people down through time, would be so counterculture, so profoundly different from society at large, such a source of amazement, that unbelievers would acknowledge it had to be supernatural. Words are cheap, but a living demonstration cannot be denied. The Spirit of Prophecy indicates that "... the strongest witness that God has sent His Son into the world is the existence of harmony and union among men of varied dispositions who form His church."[4]

Tod Bolsinger makes the following profound observation: "The church is not a helpful thing for my individual spiritual journey. The church *is* the journey. . . . The church is God's present-day word and witness to an unbelieving world. . . .

"... If you would find your life, you must lose it within a redeemed and redemptive community that together lives the manner of abundant and exceptional life that God intended for us."[5]

All other means of evangelism are secondary to visible, all-pervasive oneness. "It is absolutely crucial that Christians practice Christlike love and put an end to quarreling, harboring grudges, and struggling against one another. . . .

"... When we are divided, there is nothing we can say to which the world will pay attention."[6] *Churches that are riddled with strife or disunity are not telling the truth about the Trinity.*

One of the most powerful things we can do to reveal God to our communities is to highly value ministries within the body of Christ that focus on family life, racial harmony, conflict resolution, and relational training for our members.

As part of our emphasis on customer service, the conference treasury team chose to visit a hotel that had a reputation for relating well to its customers. The manager and event coordinator met us at 10:00 A.M. to explain their philosophy and its practical application.

The manager told us that they never use the word *customers.* They always refer to people as guests in order to create a warm, friendly atmosphere. He said, "We do everything possible to make each of our guests feel valued and cared for. In order to accomplish that we must first pay a lot of attention to building morale among our staff and teaching them how to treat one another with respect and kindness. We want every employee to feel like family. If there is division among us, our guests can tell."

He then showed us the specific materials and methods they have devised to make their goals a reality. For instance, they have designed a calendar that has one of their relational values and priorities listed on each day of the month. The calendar is accompanied by a newsletter with inspiring, real-life stories as examples. Every morning the department heads and staff meet to talk about how they can best apply that concept for that day. Each month the cycle begins over again.

In order to maintain a spirit of oneness and camaraderie among the staff, the manager models caring and support. "When I get to work in the morning," he said, "I visit the cleaning staff and kitchen personnel first, from the chefs to the dishwashers. I want to affirm them and listen to any concerns. *They* are the really important people in this hotel, you know. If I don't show up tomorrow, things will keep on running pretty well. If *they* don't show up, everything comes to a screeching halt."

He continued, "Beyond building a close-knit workforce, we also invest a lot of time and energy training the staff how to relate well to those who visit here. Each employee throughout the organization is empowered to take the initiative to immediately resolve any frustration or upset a guest may have. If, for example, a meal is not satisfactory for any reason, the waiter apologizes and then has the authority to not charge the person and to present them with a gift."

As he closed his talk, we were surprised to hear the manager say, "The event coordinator and I are both Christians, and we consider this our ministry. The importance we put on relating well to others comes from the example of our Lord." Needless to say, the hotel enjoys a wonderful reputation and has a high number of repeat guests.

Such careful attention to relational excellence and unity is the key to the church's effectiveness, as well. It will not happen by simply including it on a vision statement. It will require training and modeling, just as it did with Jesus and the Twelve. We instill confidence in the Godhead, not by the claims we make about Them but by the counterculture oneness and unity we exhibit on Their behalf.

Around the year A.D. 62 the apostle Paul picked up the theme of Jesus' John 17 prayer and chose to write a whole book of the Bible about it, called "The Letter to the Ephesians."

Under house arrest, chained to a Roman soldier for many months, Paul penned what many consider to be his loftiest, most profound teachings. Because of the way the book is constructed, the epistle was most likely intended to be read in all the churches of Asia Minor, not just in Ephesus.[7] Paul felt that the teachings of the book were of such vast importance that all the churches needed to understand them. Even though the apostle's body is confined, his mind roams freely, and the epistle is "… filled with the sense of the mighty purpose of God for His Church."[8]

The Members of the Trinity—the Father, Son, and Holy Spirit—are prominent throughout Ephesians. Paul mentions Them together several times to emphasize that whatever is being accomplished on earth spiritually is entirely due to the initiative and resources of the Godhead. To Them goes all the glory and praise.

The main theme of Ephesians is stated in the first half of chapter 1, "For he has made known to us in all wisdom and insight the mystery of his will, according to his purpose which he set forth in Christ as *a plan for the fulness of time, to unite all things in him, things in heaven and things on earth*" (Ephesians. 1:9, 10, RSV; italics supplied).

The expression "fulness of time" refers to the period between the first and second comings of Christ.[9] The Greek word translated "plan" means to administer or manage.[10] "Paul, therefore, is stating that now God has revealed to us His plan for the management of the universe. It consists in bringing together all things in Christ."[11] *The overarching intention of the Trinity, Their highest goal, is to bring into oneness in Christ all the discordant elements of the cosmos that have been torn apart by sin.*

The Godhead is eager to create oneness because it is so fundamental to Their relationships with each Other. They are attempting to replicate Their own closeness among us.

Paul then talks about a stunning development in his day that illustrated, in the most compelling manner imaginable, the power of the Trinity to accomplish Their plan. The apostle points to the fact that *Jews and Gentiles had become united in Christ.* Miraculously, Jews and Gentiles were now praying together, studying together, eating together, laughing together, and sharing their lives together.

No one could have believed such a thing was possible, because there were so many *seemingly insurmountable barriers to overcome.*

We could not imagine two groups of people who hated each other more. The deep racial animosities went back for generations. As far as the Jews were concerned, Gentiles were good for nothing but fuel for the fires of hell. It was not even lawful for a Jew to help a Gentile woman in childbirth because that would bring one more member of that detested race into the world. If a Jew married a Gentile, the Jewish parents conducted a funeral for their child because they viewed such a union as equivalent to death.[12] Signs on the outer wall of the Jewish temple warned (this is a paraphrase), *"You Gentiles can stand outside of our church and watch from a distance, but if you try to come in, WE'LL KILL YOU!"*

In order to enter into oneness with Gentiles, Christian Jews not only had to forsake their bitter hatred, but they also had to be willing to give up the elements of Jewish life that were made obsolete by the death and resurrection of Christ. Since childhood, they had been taught that circumcision, animal sacrifices, and all the rituals associated with the ceremonial law were crucial aspects of their faith. But all of that had to be left behind in order to enter into Jesus' plan of reconciliation.

For the Gentiles' part, they had to overcome mountains of mistrust and forgive all the oppression, rejection, prejudice, and abuse they had endured from Israelites for so many years. Paul says in Ephesians 2 that spiritually they also had to overcome the fact that they were "dead in . . . transgressions and sins," "separate from Christ, excluded from citizenship in Israel . . . [and] without hope and without God in the world" (verses 1, 12, NIV).

Amazingly, by the grace of God, the Jewish and Gentile believers had now become so close to each other that the apostle could say it was as if they were citizens of the same country, members of the same family, or stones used to build a glorious temple (see Ephesians 2:19–22). In privileges and opportunities they were equal in every way within the society of the church.

Paul then takes the whole experience to a much higher level by teaching that the New Testament church was not only made up of Jews and Gentiles alongside each other, but the Holy Spirit had taken the two groups and created something entirely different and unique. The apostle writes, "His purpose was to create in himself *one new man out of the two*" (Ephesians 2:15, NIV; italics supplied). ". . . Gentiles do not simply rise to the status of Jews, . . . both become something *new* and greater; . . . 'it brings into the world a new kind of thing, a new quality of thing, which did not exist before.' "[13]

John R. W. Stott adds, "It would be hard to exaggerate the grandeur of [Paul's] vision. The new society God has brought into being is nothing short of *a new creation, a new human race*, whose characteristic is no longer alienation but reconciliation, no longer division and hostility but unity and peace. This new society God rules and loves and lives in."[14] For Paul, this thrilling, miraculous reconciliation was proof that the Trinity's lofty purposes were becoming a reality, that Their vision was indeed attainable because it depended on God's power, not man's.

The challenge from Ephesians for us today is clear.

> It is simply impossible . . . to go on proclaiming that Jesus by his cross has abolished the old divisions and created a single new humanity of love, while at the same time we are contradicting our message by tolerating racial or social or other barriers within our church fellowship. . . .
>
> . . . I wonder if anything is more urgent today, for the honour of Christ and the spread of the gospel, than that the church should be seen to be, . . . a family of reconciled brothers and sisters who love their Father and love each other . . . Only then will the world believe in Christ as Peacemaker. Only then will God receive the glory due to his name.[15]

Ellen White urges, "The Lord's people are to be one. There is to be no separation in His work."[16] She also writes, "The world needs to see worked out before it the miracle that binds the hearts of God's people together in Christian love."[17]

In the spring of 1962, a young lady aged thirteen was attending a small Seventh-day Adventist eight-grade school in the United States. Even though she was the only Black child in attendance, she did not see herself as different from the other children in the school. Toward the end of the school year, she and the other eighth-grade children visited an Adventist boarding academy ninety miles from her home. She was very excited about going to the school with the rest of her friends. She wanted to meet the dean and see the girls' dorm where she would be staying.

"For the most part, while on the campus she did not feel any rejection but she was crushed when she received a letter from the school after returning home, suggesting that she should go to a school 'for her own people.' She said, 'I did not understand what they meant. I was a Seventh-day Adventist. These *are* my people.' "[18]

Such incidents are extraordinarily hurtful, and they portray to the world a terribly distorted picture of God. That incident was not an isolated experience, and even though decades have passed since it happened, we still need to determine to forsake any attitudes, of whatever nature, that threaten or destroy oneness.

In Ephesians 3, Paul writes, "[God's] intent was that now, through the church, *the manifold wisdom of God* should be made known to the rulers and authorities in the heavenly realms, according to his eternal purpose" (verses 10, 11, NIV; italics supplied).

The word translated "manifold" was normally used to describe multicolored items in everyday life such as flowers, embroidered cloth, and woven carpets. Saying that the church makes known God's *manifold wisdom* means that it "is like a beautiful tapestry. Its members come from a wide range of colourful backgrounds. No other human community resembles it. Its diversity and harmony are unique. . . . And the many-coloured fellowship of the church is a reflection of the many-coloured . . . wisdom of God."[19] The church, by definition, must look like that because it is in the reconciliation business.

Paul tells us that what happens in the church has cosmic significance, impacting the thinking of "rulers and authorities in the heavenly realms"

(Ephesians 3:10, NIV). The apostle is saying that the way church members relate to each other and their community makes a powerful statement about God to beings throughout the cosmos.

With its in-depth insights into the nature of the great controversy, our church should be foremost in cooperating with the Godhead in accomplishing Their central goal of unity in Christ. The name "Seventh-day Adventist" should be synonymous with the lowest divorce rate, the most remarkable racial harmony, the greatest gender equity, and the most profound church oneness in the world.

Unity is not uniformity. We do not all have to see things the same way. *Oneness and unity do mean* building a bond of mutual caring and respect. They mean being fully dedicated to the other person's wholeness and joy. They mean at the end of the day being committed to common goals that are larger than our individual selves.

Considering the vital importance of oneness, Paul strongly urges his readers to "*Make every effort* to keep the unity of the Spirit through the bond of peace" (Ephesians 4:3, NIV). Markus Barth comments, " 'It is hardly possible to render exactly the urgency contained in the underlying Greek verb. Not only haste and passion, but a full effort of the whole man is meant, involving his will, sentiment, reason, physical strength, and total attitude. . . Yours is the initiative! Do it now! Mean it! *You* are to do it! I mean it!—Such are the overtones in verse 3.' "[20]

The vision that Paul presents in Ephesians not only focuses on oneness within the church but also on the church's role in extending that oneness into all aspects of society. He writes, "And God placed all things under his [Christ's] feet and appointed him to be head over everything for the church, which is his body, the fullness of him who fills everything in every way" (Ephesians 1:22, 23, NIV). Christ is the Head. The church is His body. The head needs to have a body through which it can express itself.[21] William Barclay writes, "... Jesus is bit by bit filling all things in all places, and that filling is being worked out by the Church. This is one of the most tremendous thoughts in all Christianity. *It means nothing less than that God's plan for one world is in the hands of the Church.*"[22]

Physicists have discovered what they call the "laws of thermodynamics" that deal with the flow of energy in nature. The second law of thermodynamics states that left to themselves things tend toward chaos.

Society at large is like that, as well. Because of sin, human relationships tend to break down and fall into disarray unless acted upon by some outside force. The most powerful resource God has provided to bring harmony and unity is the church. *To accomplish the Godhead's wishes, the church should not only be an example of oneness but needs to reach out proactively into all the fractured elements of society to foster unity, as well.* As the apostle wrote, "All this is from God, who reconciled us to himself through Christ and gave us the ministry of reconciliation" (2 Corinthians 5:18ff, NIV).

An inspiring example of this type of church-based reconciliation ministry is the existence of "Shalom Communities." (*Shalom* being Hebrew for "peace.") Marianne Comfort explains.

> In April of 1992, Los Angeles exploded in riots and looting when white police officers were acquitted in the videotaped beating of black motorist Rodney King. On the other side of the country, religious leaders gathered for a national meeting and bowed their heads.
>
> The riots triggered some deep soul-searching at the United Methodist Church's general conference in Louisville, Ky. Upon hearing the news, the 1,000 delegates prayed for an answer to urban despair and violence.
>
> The solution they arrived at they called "shalom communities"—a biblical vision of spiritual, physical and emotional well-being. The Methodists decided to focus on small geographic areas, often only a few city blocks, with the goal of combining spiritual, social and economic renewal.
>
> Now, five years later, more than 150 shalom zones dot the United States. . . .
>
> What's new, participants say, is that these churches are now consciously focusing on building relationships of trust among

> disparate racial, ethnic and economic groups—in addition to tackling concrete neighborhood improvement projects. …
>
> Tenant-landlord disputes that once ended in frustration and occasional violence are now mediated by a church worker familiar with the community. Police citations against street vendors and health department raids on home-based food businesses—which reinforced residents' distrust of authorities—are now worked out through dialogue that deliberately attempts to bridge cultural differences. …
>
> Now, [Rev. Jim] Hamilton said, in his neighborhood, "there's a sense of calm more than there's ever been."[23]

It is up to each local Seventh-day Adventist church to discover how the Trinity wants them to become a source of relational healing in their own community. There are myriad opportunities if we only watch and listen.

Some might say that we should not get involved in "social issues." Preaching the gospel by itself will indeed reach a certain segment of society, but the good news will ring hollow for the vast majority unless they first see us rolling up our sleeves and doing everything we can in very practical ways to address the brokenness and alienation of their world. We need to assert Jesus' Lordship not only over individual hearts but also over all the aspects of society fractured by sin. In hurting neighborhoods, dirty hands garner far more credibility than holy words.

Once I began more fully to comprehend the Trinity's plan, the Holy Spirit led me to examine ways in which I myself was being a source of disunity. Sad to say, I could identify far too many times over the years when in our family, for instance, I was critical, selfish, and demanding, times that brought tension and upset.

After I understood the Godhead's passion for oneness in John 17 and Ephesians, I realized that my actions were painting a horrible picture of God and that I was, in fact, working directly against Heaven's purpose. I earnestly asked the Holy Spirit to change me and am now trying to learn each day how, by the grace of God, to be a more effective agent of harmony and oneness in my world.

In Ephesians 1:17, 18 the apostle Paul writes, "... I couldn't stop thanking God for you—every time I prayed, ... But I do more than thank. I ask—ask the God of our Master, Jesus Christ, the God of glory—to make you intelligent and discerning in knowing him personally, your eyes focused and clear, *so that you can see exactly what it is he is calling you to do, [and] grasp the immensity of this glorious way of life he has for Christians*" (*The Message;* italics supplied).

You have been called to participate in the most important, most challenging, most gratifying endeavor ever entrusted to humankind. You have been invited to partner with the Godhead in the accomplishment of a dream They have had ever since sin began—a dream of replicating the oneness within the Trinity by bringing all things in heaven and earth into oneness in Christ. Through your words and deeds, in the home, church, community, and workplace, you can be an ambassador of reconciliation and relational healing to fractured, broken, disenfranchised lives.

Helen Keller once wrote, "I am only one; but still I am one. I cannot do everything, but still I can do something." "... I will not refuse to do the something that I can do."[24]

---

1 See Ellen G. White, *The Ministry of Healing,* p. 52.

2 Woodrow Whidden, Jerry Moon, and John W. Reeve, *The Trinity* (Hagerstown, Md.: Review and Herald®, 2002), p. 123.

3 Ibid., pp. 20, 153, 243.

4 Ellen G. White, *The Acts of the Apostles,* p. 549.

5 Tod E. Bolsinger, *It Takes a Church to Raise a Christian,* pp. 17, 18; italics in original.

6 Ray C. Stedman, *Body Life* (Grand Rapids, Mich.: Discovery House Publishers, 1972), p. 52.

7 See William Barclay, *The Letters to the Galatians and Ephesians* (Philadelphia: The Westminster Press, 1976), p. 70.

8 Francis Foulkes, *The Epistle of Paul to the Ephesians* (Grand Rapids, Mich.: Eerdmans, 1978), p. 16.

9 *The Seventh-day Adventist Bible Commentary* (Washington, D.C.: Review and Herald®, 1957), 6:1000.

10 Francis Foulkes, *The Epistle of Paul to the Ephesians,* p. 52.

11 Homer A. Kent Jr., *Ephesians: The Glory of the Church* (Chicago: Moody Press, 1971), p. 24.

12 William Barclay, *The Letters to the Galatians and Ephesians,* p. 107.

13 Francis Foulkes, *The Epistle of Paul to the Ephesians,* p. 83; italics in original.

14 John R. W. Stott, *The Message of Ephesians: God's New Society* (Downers Grove, Ill.: InterVarsity Press, 1979), p. 110; italics supplied.

15 John R. W. Stott, *The Message of Ephesians: God's New Society,* pp. 111, 112.

16 Ellen G. White, *Testimonies for the Church,* 8:165.

17 Ellen G. White, *God's Amazing Grace,* p. 211.

18 Michael F. Cauley, paper for class in Historical Studies in Executive Leadership, McCormick Theological Seminary, September 2004; interview with Erica Scott Wright; italics supplied.

19 John R. W. Stott , *The Message of Ephesians: God's New Society,* p. 123.

20 Ibid., p. 154; italics in original.

21 William Barclay, *The Letters to the Galatians and Ephesians,* p. 93.

22 Ibid.; italics in original.

23 Marianne Comfort, " 'Shalom' Zones Give New Spirit to Urban Renewal," American News Service, June 16, 1997. From http://www.villagelife.org/news/archives/6-16-97_shalomzones.html, Dec. 20, 2006.

24 Helen Keller, quoted on http://quotations.home.worldnet.att.net/helenkeller.html, Dec. 20, 2006.

Chapter 9

Diversity

At some point in time, God made five hundred separate body parts and told them to join together to become ten people. He showed them a portrait He had drawn of what a complete person should look like. He also said they needed to come together as soon as possible in order to find food to eat or else they'd die. Then He left.

All of the parts immediately began to look around and size up the others. At first, the only thing a lone right hand could see were five stomachs that happened to be laying nearby. He looked at himself and then at his neighbors and didn't see any resemblance at all. He felt odd and insecure and began to wonder if there was something wrong with him . . . or them.

He strained to see farther and spotted what he thought was another right hand about three feet away. Overjoyed, he slowly flopped his way over and greeted the right hand warmly.

"Boy, am I glad to see you," he said.

His new friend replied, "Yeh, I'm really happy to see you too." He pointed to the three eyeballs that were mere inches away and whispered, "Those things look *so-o-o-o* weird. Super white with that small, dark area in the middle. They've been staring at me for the last five minutes. Spooky. I don't know if any of them can be trusted."

Eventually all the hands found each other. They huddled off to one side, and someone made a motion that they start a "Hand Division" for mutual support. When the floor was opened for discussion, a left hand spoke up, "I don't mean to be picky, but I've noticed that half of us have the thumb on the left side and the other half on the right. For the sake of complete harmony, I would like to amend the motion to have us develop *two* Hand Divisions—one for right and one for left." The measure passed unanimously.

While all this was going on, the other body parts chose to huddle with their own kind as well—brains with brains, legs with legs, hearts with hearts, and so on.

One member of the liver group observed, "Only a liver can really understand the needs of another liver." A chorus of "right on" went up from the other livers.

"All the various parts act so differently," a kidney commented. "Take those noses over there. I can't imagine spending all day sniffing like that. I could never feel comfortable hanging around those things. And the hearts—beating, beating, beating, beating. It would drive me *crazy* if I had to be connected to a part that can't sit still for two seconds. How could I get any sleep at night! No way."

After a couple of hours, a rumor began to circulate that the brains were on a "power trip." "They're just a bunch of know-it-alls," a spleen complained. "Pushy too."

Another organ added, "I think the spinal chord's in on it, as well."

"The nerve!" a foot gasped.

Several groups of organs signed a petition demanding that there be equal authority for all. "Give those brains half an inch and they'll take a mile," was the general sentiment.

By the second morning, all the body parts were complaining about being hungry. The stomachs kept making annoying growling sounds.

"What are we going to do?" worried a pancreas.

Another pancreas responded, "I don't mean to sound like a trouble-maker or anything, but I think we need to put ourselves together and make actual people like God told us."

Several other groups caught the spirit. Ideas started flying. The new "Let's Make People" movement held a rally. Speeches and cheers followed. Momentum grew, and within an hour all of the groups were on-board. Driven by hunger, different parts came together according to whom they felt most comfortable with or who happened to be nearest. For ten long hours they struggled to rearrange themselves.

"OK," an elbow urged, "now let's look around for some food." But they couldn't go anywhere because no two parts were in the right place.

By the fifth day everyone was desperate. "We gotta have food," complained the esophagus. "I'm feeling really weak."

On the sixth day, the small intestine spoke up. "Quiet, everyone! Quiet! Anyone seen that picture of a complete body that God showed us? What happened to that thing? We should've used that to start with."

"Yeah, almost forgot about that," the large intestine added. "Gotta be around here somewhere."

Starvation sparked a general search, with parts flopping and dragging themselves in every direction.

After a while, the thyroid shouted, "I got it! I got it! It was under some leaves."

Everyone huddled around, studying the plan earnestly. Just as predicted, the brains soon took over, but no one complained. "Look," they instructed, "from what we see on God's plan, none of this can work unless you stop hanging around your own group all the time."

"Hands, get together with the arms," the brains directed. "Legs, according to God's plan you're with the feet and hips. Spine, link up with the rib cage. Neck, we need you here with us." They directed the "internal organs" to link up and coordinate. On and on it went. At one point the brains got upset at the ears for insisting they belonged on the back of the head. But overall, everything went remarkably well.

Then came the moment of truth. The brains shouted, "Everyone, stand up." Awkwardly at first, then with more confidence, hands pushed off from the ground, heads looked up, torsos became upright, and ten pairs of legs extended. With a final push, there, amazingly, stood ten fully formed human beings. A big cheer went up from all the parts, although the "internal organs" were a little muffled within the chest cavity. All ten human beings joined hands and cried for joy. They immediately started picking berries and plucking apples and pears and every imaginable food.

The apostle Paul spoke to the same issues and problems highlighted in this parable when he wrote, "The body is a unit, though it is made up of many parts; and though all its parts are many, they form one body. . . . If the foot should say, 'Because I am not a hand, I do not belong to the body,' it would not for that reason cease to be part of the body. . . . If the whole body were an eye, where would the sense of hearing be? ... But in fact God has arranged the parts in the body, every one of them, just as he wanted them to be. . . . Now you are the body of Christ, and each one of you is a part of it" (1 Corinthians. 12:12–27, NIV). The great diversity within the human body illustrates the wonderful diversity within the body of Christ. Such diversity is God-ordained, and only under His guidance and leadership can it function effectively.

Paul then says that the various body parts represent spiritual gifts given to us by God (see 1 Corinthians 12). By my count, at least twenty gifts appear in Scripture, and every Christian is guaranteed to have at least one. These special abilities, combined with all of our other talents and attributes, enable us to fulfill our unique role in the church. You are a one-of-a-kind person.

In addition to spiritual gifts, diversity within the body of Christ also involves culture, race, ethnic groupings, gender, age, and temperaments. In the eyes of God, such diversity is a great strength, a precious gift to be highly valued.

We can learn certain lessons about diversity that can help us greatly in our attempts to implement the church's purpose of reflecting the Trinity.

Lesson 1: The purpose of diversity is unity, not division

Paul again employs the body analogy in Ephesians, where he teaches that our diversity was given "so that the body of Christ may be built up *until we all reach unity in the faith* . . . and become mature, attaining to the whole measure of the fullness of Christ" (Ephesians 4:12, 13, NIV italics supplied).

If we look only to our own needs, we will be divided. We may claim to be unified simply because we are all "body parts," but true unity only comes when we look beyond our own needs and desires and focus on how we can humbly serve one another in the Spirit of Christ.

A teacher in a fourth-grade class introduced a game called "balloon stomp." A balloon was tied to each child's ankle, and the object was to pop everybody else's balloon while protecting your own. The last person standing with an un-popped balloon wins.

"… A few of the children hung shyly on the sidelines, but their balloons were doomed just the same. The battle was over in a matter of seconds. Only one balloon was still inflated, and, of course, its owner was the most disliked kid in the room."

A second class was brought in to play the same game. The only difference was that these children were mentally handicapped. The teacher gave the same instructions but gave them too quickly for these children to grasp clearly. All they understood was that balloons were supposed to be popped. They then got the idea on their own that they were supposed to *help each other* pop balloons.

"… So they formed a kind of balloon stomp co-op. One little girl knelt down and held her balloon carefully in place, like the holder for a field-goal kicker, while a little boy stomped it flat. Then he knelt down and held his balloon still for her to stomp. On and on it went, all the children helping one another in the Great Stomp."

When the final balloon was popped, everyone cheered. Everybody had won.

"The question you have to ask is, who got the game right, and who got the game wrong?

"The question you have to answer is, which game are you going to play?"[1]

Cooperation and mutual support equal life. Separation equals death—not physical death but death to the Trinity's vision of what we can become together in Their power and under Their leadership. Diversity in the hands of human beings creates division. Diversity in the hands of God creates divinely inspired unity.

Lesson 2: Diversity makes it easier for unbelievers to accept Christ

Jesus said, "If you are friendly only to your friends, how are you different from anyone else? Even the heathen do that" (Matthew 5:46, 47, TLB).

To be the witness to the world that God intended, church needs to be made up of people that society couldn't imagine ever coming together as one. For church to be seen as a miracle by nonbelievers, it actively must seek out and embrace people from different races, cultures, backgrounds, temperaments, personalities, and ages. The greater the differences, the more miraculous the oneness. And the greater the miracle, the more likely it is that nonbelievers will admit that Jesus' claims to being humankind's Redeemer must be true.

Lesson 3: It is in diversity that I find my identity

Each of us is like one piece in a large puzzle. My life finds its identity in relation to all the other puzzle pieces. Together we form a wonderful picture. In spiritual terms, we form a beautiful picture of God.

"... I am uniquely me in the presence of others who need me to complement and fulfill the total picture we become together. None of us takes on the other's identity. Together we become what we could not become alone. It is God's unique plan that it be so."[2]

Shortly after entering seventh grade, I tried out for junior varsity football. Making the team was a matter of great import with me because I desperately wanted to follow in the highly athletic footsteps of my dad. He had been a "twelve letter man," earning a varsity letter in three sports during each year of high school. It was a remarkable achievement, and I was determined to carry on his legacy.

Try-outs were held over a two-day period. Unfortunately they couldn't find a uniform small enough for my undersized body. So, the football pants hung ignominiously down around my ankles (instead of my knees), the number on the back of my jersey was half tucked in, and the helmet covered my eyes whenever I bent over. But what I lacked in stature I made up for in grit and determination. When the roster was finally posted, I scanned it nervously. To my great relief my name appeared right there along with those of my close friends, Johnny Parker, Dean Perry, and Sherman Shuck.

That week the coach gave each of us our assignment, based on how he had assessed us at practice. I was a defensive end.

I'll never forget the first time the coach yelled out my name. "Johnson, get in there!" Our team was kicking off, and I lined up where I'd been taught. I got down in the classic football stance, which caused the helmet to fall down over my eyes. Not being able actually to see the kick-off, I waited until I heard it, then ran furiously down the field. I felt the full weight of my dad's exploits resting on my narrow shoulders as I sped along the turf. Suddenly, I saw the ball carrier turn in my direction. I dove for his thick, hairy legs and hung on for dear life until reinforcements arrived. Within moments other players piled on and toppled the runner. A broad smile broke out on my mud-stained face.

I still look back on that season with great fondness. I can hear the metallic clacking from the cleats on our football shoes hitting the cement floor as we stomped out of the locker room. I can smell the blended aroma of dirt, sweat, line chalk, and freshly mown grass. I recall the banter and joking on the school bus as we traveled to away games. I can hear the cheers for a well-run play and the words of encouragement when someone failed.

The only way I could understand my role as a defensive end was to see how I fit in with the rest of the team. It was only in relation to what everyone else was doing that I could visualize what I was supposed to do.

As in football, I come to understand the role I am to play in the church by seeing myself in relation to how the Holy Spirit is calling others. How I fit in becomes clearer when I see myself in relation to the diverse whole.

Lesson 4: Diversity is a source of personal growth

My own understanding is broadened by hearing other points of view. I comprehend more fully the great variety and complexity within the character of God as I interact with the variety that exists among human beings made in His likeness. Superiority vanishes in the presence of other cultures that are equally rich.

I am challenged as my own values, priorities, and approaches to life come in contact with those of others that may be even more satisfying and effective. I am encouraged to make new friends and enter new experiences as I realize that people different from me are not a threat but simply fellow human beings. I am made whole by diverse ministries on my behalf.

Lesson 5: Diversity enables individuals to become something entirely new and special

Because we are all so different and can contribute in such a wide variety of ways, we can experience what is called "synergy"—the total is more than the sum of the parts. When you put all the body parts together, you have more than simply a collection of organs, more than a stomach and lungs and kidneys arranged in a certain way. You have something entirely new—a thinking, feeling *person,* who can offer hugs and a helping hand. The same can be said of the church because it is more than a collection of individuals. It is the body of Christ through which He can continue His ministry of love.

Lesson 6: Christ was so committed to diversity because diversity is integral to the Trinity itself

We serve one God, but there are Three distinct Persons with different roles. That, then, becomes the model for the church.

Donald Macleod writes, "Enough has been said, one hopes, to establish the importance of the doctrine of the Trinity for the unity of the church. But it is no less important for the church's diversity. We have seen that the Father, the Son and the Spirit are clearly distinct. Each is different. Each has his own unique quality which gives him his personal identity. If the church is to reflect the life of the Trinity it must do justice to this diversity. We are not only to concede that Christians are all different. We are to insist on it and even to revel and take pride in it."[3]

During His earthly ministry, Jesus yearned to create diversity among His followers by bringing together people from every imaginable background. For Him, diversity was an imperative, a way of life.

One of the main reasons the Savior continually got into hot water was because of the kinds of friends He made. He kept bringing people to church who no one thought belonged in church.

Without doubt Christ's most over-the-top friendships were with pork-eating, idol-worshiping non-Jews. As soon as the Lord found someone who was from a different race, culture, background, or way of life, He said, "Oh, we've *got* to have you around. You would add *so* much to who we are." Jesus was like a painter constantly searching for new colors to use on his palette.

Christ was, after all, the Creator who at the beginning of this world was not content with twenty varieties of flowers, not even a hundred, but thousands, from begonias to roses. He wasn't content with fifty types of birds but made a profusion of different shapes and sizes and colors, from robins to eagles.

One afternoon the Savior told a story that blew the roof right off the diversity-resisting Jewish mind-set of His day. Christ was a captivating storyteller, and the Jewish authorities listened in spite of themselves. It was a simple tale of ambush and rescue.

Jesus said, " 'A certain man went down from Jerusalem to Jericho, and fell among thieves' " (Luke 10:30, NKJV). A priest passes by. A Levite passes by. Well, every profession can have a few bad apples. But . . . the hero is . . . someone the Jews absolutely hated with a passion, a Samaritan!

Christ could really poke His thick carpenter's finger in someone's eye when He thought it would help them get spiritually unstuck. This was a doozie. It was later rumored that Jesus stayed in Samaritans' homes—a lot. As a member of the Trinity, Christ longed to do whatever He could to help people embrace diversity and value inclusiveness.

The Seventh-day Adventist Church currently finds itself struggling with two very significant aspects of diversity in church life. One is regional conferences administered by African Americans and the other is women's ordination. Both of these issues can evoke strong opinions and emotions.

Regional conferences were established in the mid-1940s as a result of the deep-seated prejudice that oppressed and marginalized Black members and pastors within the Seventh-day Adventist Church in North America. There were two main issues involved, among many others: leadership and resources.

It was, tragically, very difficult for qualified black pastors to enter leadership positions in the denomination at the conference level and above. Qualified individuals were often passed over, resulting in discouragement, hurt, and distrust. Without access to leadership, Blacks could not give direction to the work among their own churches or to evangelistic outreach among African Americans. Neither could they have adequate input regarding the allocation of personnel and financial resources. As a result, tensions escalated, and the work among African Americans suffered.

The many instances of racism against Black members within the Adventist Church during that time should grieve every member's heart. Far be it for me to say that I understand what our Black members endured. Only the victims themselves can fully understand.

Since the formation of regional conferences, in which Black pastors can attain administrative and departmental positions, the work among African Americans has greatly expanded. Much good has clearly been accomplished through powerful gospel preaching, effective social ministries, and other means of outreach. They have served an important purpose.

Sadly, because we have never worked through and resolved many of the underlying issues that gave birth to regional conferences, prejudice, tension, and mistrust remain a serious problem. During my thirty years as an Adventist, I have seen little coordination between churches in the state conferences and regional conferences, even when they are located in the same area. I have witnessed only a few situations in which leaders from the different conferences chose to collaborate or strategize together. I am not aware of many initiatives currently being undertaken to build bridges between the two. This reality should concern *all* church members and leaders at *all* levels. If one part of the body of Christ is hurting, all should hurt.

I feel compelled to call us to prayerfully consider this issue in relation to what the Scriptures and Spirit of Prophecy say is the central purpose of the Seventh-day Adventist Church—*to reveal the Trinity to the world.* It is vital that church life be an accurate reflection of Trinity life. The great controversy raises this issue to the highest possible priority.

My deep concern is that by maintaining separate organizations based on race, we as a total organization are portraying a distorted picture of God. In order for us to be faithful to our end-time role, the oneness within the Trinity must be the model for oneness within the church. From my perspective, this vision, this truth, should take precedence over every other consideration.

I earnestly pray that God will raise up champions for His vision among all races within our church, especially among the younger generation of Adventists, who will step forward to make their voices heard and urge that leaders open a constructive dialogue, plead with God for wisdom, and humbly work through the wrenching issues so that His name may be glorified. All conferences should share equal responsibility in finding a way to come together. An appeal also needs to go out to local churches to lead the way by intentionally establishing many multiracial congregations across the United States.

The Methodist Church in the United States has struggled with the issue of race relations as we have, and through tears, repentance, and Spirit-inspired commitment made some remarkable progress toward denomination-wide inclusion. I especially appreciate this statement from several prominent Black leaders: "The Methodist Church has now arrived at a point in its history, and in the history of the world, when our Church must become a prominent witness, within its own institutional life, to the principles of equality, brotherhood and 'oneness of all Christians in Christ,' which have been affirmed as essential elements of the Christian faith."[4]

Another polarizing diversity issue within our church is women's ordination. Thankfully, women are currently authorized to perform essentially all of the same duties as an ordained pastor. The problem, however, is that their giftedness and calling are not fully recognized by the church through official ordination to the gospel ministry equal to that of their male counterparts. It is like allowing a woman to graduate from medical school and later commending her for doing excellent surgery but refusing to officially recognize her as a physician.

The issue is not "women's lib" or an unseemly clamoring for "rights." The central concern once again is the distorted picture we are painting of the Trinity. However a person interprets Scripture on this subject, if their conclusion does not mirror the full equality found within the Godhead itself, it cannot be correct. There is no inequality at all among the Father, Son, and Holy Spirit.

It is strange that a people who give such prominence to a woman as their founder should assign women pastors to a lesser classification. It is strange that a people who insist that Adventists in widely divergent cultures around the world stop eating unclean meats should hesitate to urge the far more important issue of equality.

The issue should not be cast as a choice between unity and women's ordination.

The choice that needs to be made is to find a new type of unity that does not insist on unanimity on every issue and allows for new, fully inclusive life to emerge. We cannot afford to allow our prophetic voice of reform, that has so effectively called those outside the church to a higher plane, find itself muted within our own ranks.

In both the matter of separate conferences based on race and women's ordination, the true measure of whether we have achieved the oneness and equality God intended is not how *we* feel about it but how *unbelievers* evaluate it.

There are times in life when I am poignantly reminded of the promise that diversity holds. One of the most memorable altar calls I have ever witnessed occurred in the Primary tent at a camp meeting, with children ages six to ten. My wife and I were the overall leaders. Our usual evening schedule was to have some kind of interesting demonstration followed by a speaker or storyteller. For the demonstrations, we had a potter actually making pottery the first night. Some animals were brought in from a nearby shelter on night two. The third evening featured a performance of the gymnastics team from the nearby college. The kids sat glued to that show. After the half-hour routine, the performers pushed all of their equipment to the back of the tent behind the backdrop where they would pick it up later.

The evening speaker followed with a talk about the dedication and courage of the boy David in the Old Testament. At the end, the pastor chose to make an altar call. With keyboard music playing, he appealed, "If any of you children would like to tell Jesus 'I want to be as dedicated as David, I want to be courageous like he was,' just get up from your chairs and walk on down and join me here for prayer." Children from various places got up and responded. He repeated the call with a slight variation. More walked forward.

I was scanning the audience to keep a lid on any misbehavior, when suddenly I noticed some activity at the back of the tent, in a dimly lighted area about twenty or more feet behind the pastor. I moved to one side and looked more carefully.

Apparently, after the children arrived up front, they had spotted the gymnast's trampoline. To my surprise, the kids were bouncing gleefully. More and more were climbing up. With the music playing loudly, we couldn't hear any noise, but the children were having a ball, joining hands and springing up and down, rolling alongside each other, seeing who could jump the highest.

Oblivious to the collective delight behind him, the speaker made one last call then offered closing prayer. Afterward, as I made my way toward the trampoline to settle things down, I couldn't help but smile. The thought occurred to me, *That's it. That's what church needs to be—all of us adults, with all of our different backgrounds, responding in faith, like little children, to God's call, and then discovering unexpected togetherness and joy.*

---

1 John Ortberg, *Love Beyond Reason* (Grand Rapids, Mich.: Zondervan, 1998), pp. 151, 152.

2 Julie A. Gorman, *Community That Is Christian*, p. 19.

3 Donald Macleod, *Shared Life: The Trinity and the Fellowship of God's People*, p. 78.

4 W. Astor Kirk, *Desegregation of the Methodist Church Polity* (Pittsburgh: RoseDog Books, 2005), p. 100.

Chapter 10

The Purpose of Our Doctrines

Big corporations will often choose a catchy slogan to sum up who they are or why they exist, to use in their advertising. Knowing that the public has the attention span of a fruit fly, these companies wisely portray themselves in a brief, carefully chosen phrase. For instance:

FedEx. *"When it absolutely, positively has to be there overnight."* The FedEx slogan shouts "reliability," that you can count on them. It says they understand your needs. They care enough that they are not going to mess up. They will do whatever it takes and be quick about it. They are committed to handling your most important documents and packages with great care and efficiency.

Mark Tatge, in his article "Start the Ground War," talks about FedEx's response to the terrorist attacks on the World Trade Center. "An hour after the shutdown of the nation's commercial airspace on Sept. 11, FedEx Corp.'s global operations chief, Jack Muhs, was in a teleconference with 120 of his managers across the world. FedEx planes had delivered packages in the face of hurricanes, volcano eruptions, and labor strikes. But this was new territory. 'We couldn't just let the packages sit,' says Muhs. 'We didn't know how long the air system would be shut down.'

"Solution: trucks. But carrying 3 million express packages would require 2,085 long-haul trucks, nearly 800 more than FedEx had on hand. While the company's 235 U.S. jets sat parked on the tarmac for two days, executives hit the phones. 'We went out and leased or borrowed everything we could,' says Frederick W. Smith, FedEx's chief executive. Within 12 hours 70 percent of the packages were moving; by the next day, 100 percent. Delivery time for packages from Seattle to New York: two days."[1] That's commitment!

The Red Cross. "*We're in Your Neighborhood Every Day.*" The "we're" says that many people are involved in taking care of you. The word "neighborhood" is much more personal than, say, "geographic area." And the phrase doesn't say neighborhoods in general. The Red Cross is involved where *you* live. Finally, they are not going to just help and then take off. They are going to be there every day, around the clock, as long as is needed. The Red Cross is legendary for emergency response and practical assistance.

What do you think would be a good slogan for the Seventh-day Adventist Church? When I ask members what they think is our main purpose, why the church exists, the most common answers I get are:

"To share the truth."

"To preach the three angels' messages."

"To tell people about the second coming of Christ."

"To teach our distinctive doctrines."

"To spread the good news of the gospel."

A phrase that would summarize these responses might be, *"We will teach you correct and truthful biblical information."* That information would include all of our twenty-eight fundamental beliefs, from salvation to the Sabbath.

I am very grateful for the truth-filled information that we possess and share. I did not grow up as a Seventh-day Adventist and am the only Adventist in my family. The truths I heard and studied have given me hope and purpose.

I have worked for the denomination for thirty-plus years and have dedicated my life to serving the church and sharing truth, sometimes in ways that were so far outside my comfort zone I couldn't even see the zone anymore. One memorable example was my stint as a student colporteur.

One spring a literature evangelism leader came to visit me in my dorm room at an Adventist college. He said, "I think it would really enhance your ministerial training if you sold religious books this summer. The Savior is coming soon, and there are souls who need to read about the truths these books contain." I chose to sign on.

Starting that June, I hit the pavement. In reality I couldn't sell peanuts to an elephant. But there I was, dressed in a brown hand-me-down suit and clutching my satchel, which contained a colorful plastic fold-out display, a prospectus, and a copy of my canvass (selling points). I hadn't fully memorized the canvass by opening day but had got the gist.

At the end of the first day I found myself shouting at a bent-over, hard-of-hearing, agitated elderly lady through her locked screen door.

"Books! I'm selling books!" I bellowed.

"What?"

"BOOKS! Truth-filled r-e-a-d-i-n-g!"

"What meeting?"

"No, ma'am, I'm from the Home Health Education Service. I—"

"Whatever you're selling, mister," she interrupted, "I don't want any. You shouldn't come around scaring old people." She glowered at me suspiciously with large bloodshot eyes and then furrowed her brow and disappeared inside.

At the end of the first month, I was exhausted and discouraged. Too many shouting matches. Too many pit bulls. Too many "No way" responses. With weeks to go.

At one point, and I think I may have made history here, I actually had *negative* net sales. How? Well, I gave away far too many dollar books in an attempt to redeem countless turndowns.

The following spring, another literature evangelism leader visited my dorm room. I was reluctant but eventually caved. Another long, hot summer of knocking on doors.

I have great respect for the publishing work. It is not my cup of tea, but neither is nursing, and that is certainly a worthwhile profession, as well. These dedicated workers place truthful, life-giving information in as many homes as possible.

A decade later, in the late 1970s, I had the privilege of pastoring a small church in Massachusetts for more than six years. It was actually an old converted house with a unique, turreted, castlelike tower on one side that made it look as if it had just leaped off the pages of a *Watchtower* magazine. (I eventually took a chain saw to the thing.)

One year the congregation decided to hold evangelistic meetings and share the truths that meant so much to them. They hadn't held any such meetings in two decades. I convinced a friend to do the preaching for the series, which would be held in the little church itself. To spruce it up for anticipated guests, we painted the foyer. Then the sanctuary looked terrible; so, we painted that. That made the fellowship hall look awful; so, we painted it. That made the kitchen look really awful; so, we painted it too.

On opening night, ten non-Adventists showed up and stayed throughout. At the end they *all* chose to be baptized! The church building had no baptistry; so, I imported a mobile one. We were told the ungainly, collapsible box and thick blue liner weighed a ton when filled with H_2O, so the decision was made to reinforce several of the fellowship hall's tired floor joists. We figured that falling through the floor might discourage some of the new members.

On the big night, the church was packed. The conference president even showed up to rejoice with us.

Our entire denomination has made an enormous commitment to getting the word out, to spreading truth around the world. We are intensely dedicated to media ministries that beam the biblical information over the airways into every nook and cranny of society. Shortwave radio stations catapult the information into regions that don't have regular radio coverage. Evangelistic meetings and seminars are highly valued at every level of church organization.

As vital and important as biblical information is, a serious downside unfortunately can develop in local congregations if that information is not handled carefully. Our abundance of truth can actually present us with a significant problem when it comes to the daily workings of the church.

The problem occurs when we forget that truth was intended to be a means to an end *and not an end in itself.* Biblical information was never meant by God to be the sum of Adventism. It was always intended to be the means of attaining something much larger, a more expansive destiny, a much greater purpose.

In Jesus' day, the Pharisees had expanded the Ten Commandments to a total of six hundred and thirteen.[2] Matthew tells us that one of the Pharisaical lawyers, hoping to trap the Savior, asked Him which one of those six hundred–plus laws was most important. Without a moment's hesitation, Christ responded, " 'You shall love the Lord your God with all your heart, and with all your soul, and with all your mind. This is the great and first commandment. And a second is like it, You shall love your neighbor as yourself. On these two commandments depend all the law and the prophets' " (Matthew 22:36–40, RSV).

The lawyer asked for one commandment and Jesus gave him two, because the two could not be separated, like the front and back of a coin. Christ taught that if you take all the information in the Old Testament, from Genesis to Malachi—all the stories, all the sermons, all the teachings—they have one supreme purpose: *to enable us to love.*[3] He made it clear to His bewildered audience that biblical information was not to be an end in itself but the means to achieving a much larger, relational goal.

The apostle Paul talked about the connection between Bible truth and life: "All scripture is inspired by God and profitable for teaching, for reproof, for correction, and for training in righteousness, that the man of God may be complete, equipped for every good work" (2 Timothy 3:16,

17, RSV). The apostle also highlighted the proper role of doctrine when he wrote, "And if I have prophetic powers, and understand all mysteries and all knowledge, and if I have all faith, so as to remove mountains, *but have not love, I am nothing*" (1 Corinthians 13:2 , RSV; italics supplied).

Ouch. You see, unless our doctrines make me a more caring, kind, considerate spouse, parent, co-worker, neighbor, citizen, and church member, then they are not fulfilling their God-intended function. Medicine that is never taken heals no one. Food that is never eaten feeds no one.

The Spirit of Prophecy observes, "… we shall force them to the conclusion that the doctrine we profess cannot be the Christian doctrine, since it does not make us kind, courteous, and respectful."[4] "If the truth we profess to believe, does not change the heart and transform the character, it is of no value to us."[5] Our teachings are intended to produce an abundance of grace and love as the dominant feature of church life.

At my first baptism as a young pastor, I stood waist-deep in the lukewarm water of the church baptistry, nervously awaiting the arrival of the teenage candidate. Camera-laden family members peered in my direction as strains of "All to Jesus I Surrender" wafted across the three hundred–seat sanctuary.

My only training to be a baptizer was what I had observed from others. Most of the baptisms I had witnessed were uneventful, except for the two near-drownings and the screamer.

Soon the deaconesses guided fourteen-year-old Rebecca down the five aqua-blue steps into the tank. I said a few words of commendation, held out my forearm for her to grasp, pronounced a blessing, and then gently lowered her down into the depths.

She came up beaming and gave me a big hug. As she turned to make her way back out, I noticed, to my horror, a clearly discernible dry spot about three inches in diameter just above her forehead. The rest of her wet auburn hair hung limply around this unbaptized, unregenerate region.

Being a 100-percent melancholic worry-wart and perfectionist, my mind raced through the theological implications of what had just occurred. Was 98 percent coverage good enough? Who knew? A feeling of failure and dread washed over me. I felt like the bumbling obstetrician who drops the first baby he delivers on the white tile of the delivery-room floor.

With no time to reflect, I reacted instinctively. As Rebecca's foot landed on the first step up, I leaned forward, cupped both hands, scooped up some water, then flung it in the direction of her head. When it hit, she glanced back in bewilderment. I'm not sure that it worked, but I did my best. She may be the only person in Adventism who was baptized and sprinkled on the very same day.

Now, many years later, I have been exploring the always challenging "So what?" question. So what difference does it really make whether a person is baptized by immersion in water or not?

I was submerged in 1968. One clear benefit was the knowledge that I followed what Scripture teaches. But, beyond that, what impact is my long-ago baptism having on my life each day? What conscious difference is it making now in the kind of person I am at home, at work, and in the community? How should someone who has been immersed live differently than someone who was not? Those questions are not mere speculation, because unless Bible teachings make a difference in how Christians live, they aren't fulfilling their function.

I firmly believe that a man has, in fact, traveled to the moon and back. I believe that the Great Wall of China stretches across a gazillion miles of undulating Asian countryside. But, to be honest, those facts don't make any difference in what kind of person I am or how I cope. When my car's transmission falls apart, I don't say to myself, "Cheer up, old boy, at least the Great Wall of China is still standing." Or when I break my arm, I don't find much encouragement in knowing that human footprints dot the lunar surface. Our doctrines can become just as irrelevant unless we comprehend their purpose.

I can hear someone worrying, "So, just as long as we feel loving, it doesn't make any difference what we believe?" No. Correct Bible doctrine is essential.

Truth matters. The greater the truth, the more fully we can understand God and learn to trust Him. The greater the truth, the more fully we can come into harmony with His will. The greater the truth, the better we comprehend the cosmic issues in the Great Controversy and the easier it is to discern falsehood and error.

The choice is never between information and relationships. One leads to the other. We need *both.* It is when we lose sight of *why* the doctrines were given that unfortunate things can happen.

Imagine a contractor who forgets that his tools are to be used to build houses, and they become an end in themselves. When he puts a big ad in the Yellow Pages, all it talks about is his power saw, his tough, lightweight hammer, easy-read measuring tape, the chisels from Austria, the screwdrivers he imported from Australia, the exquisite wrenches from Germany. He has clearly missed the point and wonders why he doesn't have very many customers!

Or imagine a brick company that, over the years, develops an exceptionally pure recipe for making bricks. The formula takes the best from what others have devised, eliminates several detrimental elements, and adds a few new ones, to come up with the most advanced, most complete, brick recipe ever devised.

Excited by their magnificent discovery, the company pours all of their available resources into marketing the new recipe. The graphic arts department utilizes a wide assortment of fonts and graphics to print the recipe. Carpentry crews manufacture exquisite frame styles to hold the prints, from traditional to art deco. Lecturers conduct seminars to acquaint townspeople with the recipe.

The problem, of course, is that a brick recipe is only useful if it is used to make actual bricks. If the company could only understand the true potential of their wonderful information, they could produce bricks to build condos, townhouses, apartment buildings, and even skyscrapers as dwelling places for multitudes. In a similar way, the doctrines of the Seventh-day Adventist Church were designed to enable people to build God-honoring lives and relate to others with Christlike love.

The link between doctrine and relationships is critical to the fulfillment of our church's mission of reflecting the life of the Trinity. The additional truths we know should make us better able to display the love that exists within the Godhead. It is the revelation of that divine love that gives God's way credibility and exposes Satan's way as a fraud.

Have you ever heard of unintended consequences? It means doing something you thought was beneficial and then having it cause bad things to happen that you never intended.

Here's an example. "In 1968, ... Vermont outlawed roadside billboards and large signs in order to protect the state's pastoral vistas. One unintended consequence was the appearance of large, bizarre 'sculptures' adjacent to businesses. An auto dealer commissioned a twelve-foot, sixteen-ton gorilla, clutching a real Volkswagen Beetle. A carpet store is marked by a nineteen-foot genie holding aloft a rolled carpet as he emerges from a smoking teapot. Other sculptures include a horse, a rooster, and a squirrel in red suspenders."[6]

Another unintended consequence can occurred when television stations decided to generate more revenue for themselves by increasing the number of commercials per show to 25 percent. As a consequence, digital video recorders appeared on the market that enable a viewer to record a show and skip the commercials. "The unintended consequence of the broadcasters' decision to increase the number of ad-minutes was that it drove viewers to find ways of avoiding ads altogether."[7]

Unintended consequences can also occur in churches as a result of making biblical information and truth an end in themselves, in making them the essence of church life. Some of the more serious problems churches can experience are:

Information can become more important than people. How we treat one another can take a backseat to how much we know. Being "right" can be more valued than being gracious and kind.

Reaping becomes paramount. Making information primary can lead us to focus almost exclusively on reaping ministries because when people are confronted with the information, they inevitably have to accept it or reject it—they have to decide "yes" or "no." Behind-the-scenes ministries whose primary focus is on the essential work of seed sowing, weeding, and watering can receive scant attention.

Church members without the reaping gifts of teaching, preaching, and evangelism feel left out and don't know where they fit in. As a result, the members become spectators, feeling undervalued and unappreciated.

Making information paramount can create an "I'm OK, you're OK" mentality. People are afraid to be open and honest because they don't want others to know that they aren't living up to all the information. We become polite but essentially closed. Members suffer in silence. As one person has observed, "Church becomes the place where we all come to be lonely together." We wear masks.

All of these unintended consequences flow tragically yet quite naturally from what I call the Information Model of being church. Our doctrines are vital and correct but until we utilize them differently, until we make a dramatic shift to a more complete, balanced model of being church, these unintended results and others will inevitably follow.

Let me ask you: If I taught someone carefully from Scripture that when you die you really die, have I given a good Bible study? If I taught them that the Sabbath is on Saturday and not Sunday, have I given an effective lesson from Scripture? If I show them convincingly that the millennium follows Jesus' second coming and lasts a thousand years, have I instructed them well? NO. Because I have not shown them specifically how those doctrines can enhance their relationship to God and their fellow human beings.

In order to attract young people, in order to retain new members and help them grow in Christ, in order to reach the masses of non-Adventists and non-Christians throughout the world, *our doctrines must be clearly relevant to life.*

If you could choose, who would you nominate from anywhere on the planet as the most *unselfish* person you know? Who is the *kindest?* Picture them in your mind's eye. I envision the pastor I interned under. He was so easy to talk to and unfailingly kind and courteous. I picture my selfless mother, who was always helping others and loved to give gifts. Generous with her time, she was a wonderful listener.

That's how Ellen White says reformers should be: "Of all the people in the world, reformers should be the *most* unselfish, the *most* kind, the *most* courteous."[8] Why would she single out reformers as the ones who should have these attributes in abundance? Because the more truth a person understands, the kinder and more caring they should be. Those who have the greatest insights into doctrine should be the ones who treat people the best.

One of the clearest indicators that someone is only a false reformer is if they are harsh, stubborn, dominating, or pushy. Such self-appointed reformers may have studied a lot of facts, but they have never studied how those facts can make them better people. " '*They are the true disciples of Christ, not who know most, but who love most.*' "[9]

Imagine an award ceremony at a prestigious university in Boston. It is a gala affair at the large, ornate campus auditorium with all of the distinguished faculty and their spouses present. At least 95 percent of the teachers have Ph.D.'s. Highest per capita in the country. The majority have taught at the school for ten years, some more than thirty.

The master of ceremonies is the university president. The award he will present is for the person who best represents the school's values and spirit. This is the first year the award is being offered, and it includes a hefty check for twenty thousand dollars. Members of the faculty have been speculating all week about who would be the recipient. In the audience, a professor of chemistry whispers to his wife, "This is really going to make someone's résumé shine."

A string quartet opens the ceremony with two classical pieces, followed by a twenty-minute speech by the mayor of the city, entitled, "The Impact One Life Can Make." The president then comes to the podium amidst expectant applause. He explains that the impetus for the award came from the Board of Trustees, who wanted to boost morale by recognizing distinguished service. The money came from a gift by a former student.

The auditorium is hushed as the president intones, "After much thought and consideration, the administration has decided that the winner of the Award for Excellence should be . . . the janitor, Freddy Stanwick." A gasp ripples across the assemblage.

The president leans over and asks his secretary to please go and get Fred, who he knows is hanging around the building so he can clean up after the meeting. Soon the back door opens and a red-faced, incredulous Fred, dressed in his dark blue janitor uniform and sneakers, is led up to the podium. The president explains that he has observed Fred for several years and in his estimation he is the kindest, most thoughtful person he has ever met. "The students love Fred because they know he'll do anything he can to help them," he says. "I've noticed students often coming to him for advice. He certainly embodies the best this campus offers."

Jesus told a story with a similar theme. There are two main characters, a Pharisee and a publican, praying in the temple. (See Luke 18:9–14.) The Pharisee is an expert on Scripture and tradition, a life-long student of the Torah. He has two doctoral degrees and a Master's in religion. The publican is a tax-collector for the hated Romans and occupies the lowest rung on the Jews' cultural ladder. He has no access to Scripture and only knows what his mother taught him and what he gleans each week at temple services.

The Pharisee has a big head, while the publican is utterly self-effacing. The Pharisee is glad when people have the privilege of being near him. The publican is simply glad for the privilege of being there at all. Jesus turns to the listening crowd and says, "And the award goes to . . . the tax collector."

It is better to have a little knowledge and be a spiritual giant than to have a lot of knowledge and be a spiritual dwarf. The best happens, of course, when much knowledge produces much love.

---

1 Mark Tatge, "Start the Ground War," available for purchase at https://www.keepmedia.com/Auth.do?extId=10022&uri=/archive/forbes/2001/1126/146.html, Dec. 26, 2006.

2 Leon Morris, *The Gospel According to Matthew* (Grand Rapids, Mich.: Eerdmans, 1992), p. 563.

3 Ibid., p. 564.

4 Ellen G. White, *Testimonies for the Church*, 6:397.

5 Ellen G. White, "Brotherly Love Needed," *Review and Herald*, Oct. 31, 1893.

6 Rob Norton, "Unintended Consequences," at http://www.econlib.org/library/Enc/UnintendedConsequences.html, Dec. 26, 2006.

7 "The Law of Unintended Consequences," unsigned column at http://www.econtentmag.com/?ArticleID=7003, Dec. 26, 2006.

8 Ellen G. White, *Gospel Workers,* p. 507; italics supplied.

9 Win Arn, Carroll Nyquist, Charles Arn, *Who Cares About Love?* (Monrovia, Calif.: Church Growth Press, 1988), p. 30; italics in original.

Chapter 11

Doctrines and Everyday Life

I love to peruse "How to" books on home improvement, probably because I'm so inept at using tools and making repairs. The books speak to some inner yearning. I was never very handy, even as a kid. My dad took it as a personal defeat if he had to call in outside help to fix anything. Usually I assisted by holding the flashlight. He would say, "Shine that light a little more to the left, Bub." (He nicknamed me Bub.) As a result of that early training, I can now aim a flashlight with uncanny accuracy.

"How-to" books on all kinds of topics sell like hotcakes. One of the more audacious titles reads, *How To: Absolutely Everything You Need to Know.* The editor's note highlights some of the contents: "Learn how to use chopsticks, breakdance, tie a trash bag, diaper a baby, and parallel park. Discover the right way to do a cartwheel, use dental floss, hammer a nail, and slice bread."[1]

Another intriguing title is *How to Speak Dog: Mastering the Art of Dog-Human Communication.* That certainly opens up a whole new area of life.

I found another dog-related book that my wife might be interested in, *How to Make Your Man Behave in 21 Days or Less Using the Secrets of Professional Dog Trainers.*

Books that help people know how to deal with anxiety, broken relationships, child rearing, family issues, intimacy problems, loneliness, depression, addictions, insufferable in-laws, suffocating debt, bewildering career choices, ornery bosses, and flabby thighs are flying off the shelves. Why? Because adulthood is a bear, and we come into it terribly ill-equipped.

Rightly understood and applied, Bible doctrines have something in common with such books. They offer powerful insights into the "how-to's" of life. That is why the Seventh-day Adventist Church was given so much truth—to show sinful, hurting human beings how to know God more deeply, how to rise above self-defeating attitudes and behaviors, and how to relate well to others. The health of the body of Christ depends on the spiritual, mental, emotional, and physical health of every part.

Our fundamental beliefs should enable us to experience the fuller dimensions of Trinity life together. They point the way for the relationships, values, and priorities within the Godhead to become a reality among us. This chapter will focus on a few of our doctrines and highlight some ways they can open up new possibilities for living.

1. Baptism

My wife and I raised our daughter in Maine, where I worked for twenty years in the conference treasury department. Besides making wonderful friends there, we enjoyed living near the sea, hiking the numerous mountain trails, and taking in the breathtaking scenery. The summers were pleasant and the fall colors spectacular. It is a great place to live.

The only two downsides were the bugs and the cold. I'm not sure, but the state bird might be the mosquito. In addition to those relentless little bloodsuckers, black flies add their own special ambiance.

Swarms of them would move with my wife and me when we walked down our street.

As far as cold is concerned, neither my wife nor I skate, ski, snowshoe, ice fish, make ice sculptures, or build snowmen; so, during the long frigid months we pretty much hibernated.

Then in 2003 I received an invitation to interview for an opening in the Florida Conference treasury department. I had first traveled to Florida in the late 1990s to give a week-long seminar at a youth camp. When I got off the plane, I could not believe what I was seeing and feeling. It was the middle of January, and everywhere I looked there was lush, green vegetation interspersed with multicolored flower beds. The temperature hovered in the high seventies.

One day earlier I had been shoveling snow, lurching on ice, and wearing fifty layers of heavy clothing. Here people were lounging about in T-shirts and shorts. It was like landing on another planet.

The thought of tossing away my snow shovel had great appeal at my advanced age; so, my wife and I decided to fly down to Florida to check out this new employment opportunity.

The job interview was scheduled for 10:00 A.M. the next day. When I awoke that morning, a sense of dread and inadequacy suddenly washed over me. I could feel the cold sweat trickle down my back and underarms. I had come from a conference of five thousand members, and Florida had fifty-six thousand! Back home I had been a little fish in a little pond, but here the pond was Lake Erie. My confidence evaporated.

The interview would be conducted by a committee made up of the three conference officers and three vice presidents. My mind shouted, *You're going to mess up big time, mister. You're going to make a big fat fool of yourself today in front of all those important people!* I visited our motel bathroom four times and gulped down some headache pills.

As He had done during other episodes of insecurity and fear, the Holy Spirit graciously reminded me of my baptism, when I had died with Christ so many years before. Immersion captures well the biblical theme of spiritual death and resurrection. We go "under" and then "come up."

We die to the old way of life and are resurrected to the new. When we come out of that watery grave, the Spirit fills us with the same kind of "resurrection life" that brought forth Jesus from the tomb.

In that Florida motel room I chose to believe that my fear was part of the old self that had been buried in the baptistry. I kept telling myself that the Holy Spirit would take charge if I just allowed Him to live out His plan within me.

As I walked into the committee room, I felt like Peter stepping out of the boat onto a restless sea. I was ushered to a seat, warm greetings were extended, and the questioning began.

To my surprise, after the first half hour I actually began to *enjoy* the experience. An hour later, when the questioning was over, I left and offered a prayer of thanks for what Christ had just done for me. The interviewers later informed me that I'd been hired.

Looking back at that experience, I realize that the key was *not* in trusting that God would enable me to be calm. Strangely enough, *the key was relinquishing the need to be calm.* Once I chose by faith to let God's resurrection life manifest itself through me in any way He saw fit, I found peace. If I was responding to His voice as best I knew how, I could leave the results with Him.

Remembering that I died spiritually at my baptism in 1968 has been immensely helpful in coping with life in general. For instance, when I'm tempted to overreact to criticism or some affront, I remember, "The old Kim certainly would have responded with hurt and anger and probably lashed out, but he's spiritually dead and gone, buried with Christ; so, how can a corpse get upset?" And then Christ raises up within me a more constructive, healing, forgiving way to approach life's circumstances. I can certainly blow it, but I'm learning.

Baptism is also about new beginnings. Whenever we fall flat on our face or blow it big time in our spiritual journey, we can mentally travel back to the day of our baptism and re-commit our lives to God now the same way we did back then. And we will again be welcomed by Christ with open arms and given renewed life in Him.

The experience of immersion was designed by God to impact our senses so fully that it could be vividly recalled in times of stress, insecurity, and failure. God intended that watery plunge to be so unusual and so engaging that it would sear itself onto our brains for the rest of our lives. We do not do justice to such a powerful purpose by simply squeezing baptism in between the opening hymn and offering during Sabbath morning worship.

2. The millennium

The millennium is the thousand-year period after Jesus' second coming when the saved inhabit heaven before returning to the new earth. For ten centuries, the Trinity will open up all the records of Their decision making since sin began.

A thousand years is a very long time. In the earthly year A.D. 1000, the world's population stood at only three hundred million. Gunpowder had just been invented in China. Leif Ericsson landed in what is today Newfoundland and called it Vinland.[2] Anyone who took five baths a year was thought by many to be a fanatic.[3] The largest city in the world back then was Cordova, Spain.[4] Try to picture living from that time until this, and you will have approximated the length of time we'll be given to quiz the Godhead.

As I write, the newspapers contain articles about a congressman from Louisiana who is accused of taking one hundred thousand dollars in bribes. He called an FBI search of the records in his congressional office an "outrageous intrusion."[5]

Because the members of the Godhead are omniscient (all knowing) and omnipotent (all powerful) you would think They, too, would say, "It's outrageous to have these puny little sinners review Our thinking and decision making. Who do these pipsqueaks think they are?" But no, just the opposite is true. Before we even asked, They took the initiative to throw open the records and invite us in.

In order to understand how the future millennium can have meaning for our lives today, we need to look behind the event itself to the heart of

God. We need to discover the underlying core value that led God to plan such an experience.

The fact that during the millennium we can ask any question and explore any concern tells us that the Trinity is fully committed to building in-depth relationships based on transparency, honesty, and trust. No hidden agendas. No deception. No false front. They are the most open, transparent Beings in the universe.

Because we are called to reflect the life of the Trinity, the millennium becomes the model for how we can build successful, fulfilling relationships *with each other now.* We need to follow the Godhead's lead and relate to those around us on the basis of honesty, openness, and trust as well. We might call that approach to life "millennial living."

Men are notoriously difficult to convince to open up. A wife asks her husband how things went at work, and he replies "Fine."

"What kinds of things did they have you doing today?"

"Same old stuff."

"How did that big meeting with the bank go?"

"No problem."

"Did you feel good about your presentation?"

"Yup."

"What did the boss say about that project you've been working on for so long?"

"Let's not get into that, OK?"

Then hubby plops down in front of the TV and reaches for the remote.

Suppose when we get to heaven at the beginning of the millennium, we ask the Trinity, "How did the plan of salvation turn out?" and They reply, "Fine."

"What kinds of things have been going on up here lately?"

"Same old stuff."

"How did it go with wrapping things up on earth at the end?"

"No problem."

"Do You feel things turned out pretty much as expected?"

"Yup."

"Could You tell us why so many people didn't make it?"

"Let's not get into that, OK?"

That kind of dialogue is not going to happen because the Father, Son, and Holy Spirit will make an intense effort to communicate. They care too much about us to clam up or keep things inside or harbor secrets. The millennium points the way as the model for new possibilities in our relationships with each other every day.

3. The Sabbath

The doctrine of the Sabbath provides several keys to developing a happy, effective relationship with God and with those around us.

a. Jesus' Lordship. What is at issue in whether we keep the Sabbath on Saturday or Sunday is the Lordship of Christ. There is nothing special that happens in nature to indicate that the Sabbath is different than any other day of the week. We don't see a rainbow in the sky every time the sun sets on Friday evening. The only reason we rest and worship on Saturday is that Jesus told us to. By keeping the biblical Sabbath, I am testifying that Christ is the ultimate Authority in my life.

The fact that the Savior wants to be my Lord is very good news because, left to myself, I am terrible at running me. Every Sabbath is a reminder of who is in charge. It takes the pressure off, because I know that Someone infinitely wiser than I am has agreed to take the reins of my life.

b. Time With God. Jesus' gift of the Sabbath reveals the importance God places on having a close relationship with each of us. He invites us to dramatically deepen our connection with Him by devoting one day a week to focusing more intensely on His love. Love for Him will inevitably strengthen our love for each other.

c. Renewal. Life can rob us of fulfillment and joy when it becomes too hectic and too demanding. We can find ourselves constantly working our way down a lengthy To Do list that never seems to end. Sabbath was designed to interrupt that debilitating lifestyle.

Aesop wrote a famous story about a goose and golden eggs. One day a poor farmer discovers a golden egg in the nest of his pet goose. Astonished, he takes the egg to be appraised and is told it's indeed pure gold. He becomes even more astonished when the same thing happens the next day and the next. Day after day, he rushes to the nest to find another golden egg and eventually becomes a very wealthy man.

Wealth, however, turns to greed and impatience. Unwilling to wait for the golden eggs, he decides to kill the goose and get them all at once. But when he opens the goose, it is empty. No more eggs, and now there will never be any more. The farmer killed the goose that laid the golden egg.[6]

Stephen Covey applies this parable to what he calls P and PC, *Production* and *Production Capacity.* "P" is the golden eggs. "PC" is the goose that laid them. So much of our energy is expended on production. We focus on what we can accomplish at home and at work. We usually spend far too little time focusing on what it takes to *produce* those results.

Covey maintains that effectiveness in life depends on maintaining a proper balance between P and PC. This means taking time to renew and deepen so that the results can be consistent and fulfilling.

The only way my car is going to have a long life is if I periodically bring it in for maintenance. I don't know very much about cars, so I just tell our trusted mechanic, "Do whatever it says in the manual." I can't just drive it without paying much attention to what it takes to keep it running well. Amazingly, the car has gone over 260,000 miles.

Unfortunately, I am not as good at maintenance in my own life. A little tape keeps running in my head that says, "Be useful, be useful." It scolds me when I take time off. On vacations I get antsy if we aren't seeing something or learning something. I have had to learn how to pay more attention to PC—production capacity.

Sabbath is all about PC. God knew our tendency toward self-destructive habits, and He provided Sabbath as a special day for spiritual, mental, and emotional renewal.

The creation of the Sabbath as a day of renewal actually points us to a core value within the Trinity that can make an impact every day of the week. Sabbath is the manifestation of an underlying principle. *It is a concrete expression of the importance the Trinity places on balanced living in general.*

Sabbath calls us away from compartmentalizing our lives and toward a more holistic perspective. It calls us to reject the segmentation of life that can lead a person, for instance, to give up meat eating yet gobble up tons of ice cream. It was compartmentalization of life that led to the imbalanced, narrow-minded thinking of the Pharisees. Jesus spent a lot of time trying to get people to focus on principles, to look at the big picture.

That broader perspective would indicate that we are not living in harmony with Heaven's plan when we kill ourselves all week and crash on Saturday. We may keep the day but ignore the value system that gave birth to the day. We may refrain from work on Sabbath but ignore the philosophy of life it symbolizes. To be a good Sabbath keeper, I need to pay attention to balanced living as a way of life.

d. Making Time for Relating. By building a Sabbath into our relationship with Him, God modeled a key aspect of all healthy relationships, both in marriage and in other aspects of life. He demonstrated that in-depth relationships cannot be developed with a meager personal investment or leftover energy. *Sabbath highlights the underlying principle that building relationships takes time.* If we apply that principle properly, we not only will spend time with God on Sabbath but all during the week.

Likewise, God's example calls us not only to be with family and friends on Saturday but also to build quantity time with them into the other days of the week. It calls a husband to schedule regular dates with his wife. It calls parents to schedule family nights without TV and to eat supper together at the table. It calls us to make time to invest in each other. In that way, the values that Sabbath represents permeate all of life. It is those values that drive our schedules and not the other way around.

4. The Investigative Judgment

Adventists believe that after Jesus' resurrection, He began His mediatorial work in heaven. As indicated by the prophecies of Daniel, the "cleansing of the sanctuary" began in 1844. At that time Christ entered the investigative judgment phase of His ministry. In many ways, this momentous time is to the unfallen worlds what the millennium will later be to the redeemed.

In the investigative judgment our individual lives will ultimately come up for review in the heavenly realm. If we have turned our lives over to Jesus, we have nothing to fear. The case will be decided on His merits, not ours. We can have full assurance that all will be well. "There is therefore now no condemnation to those who are in Christ Jesus" (Romans 8:1, NKJV). "Rest in God. He is able to keep that which you have committed to Him. If you will leave yourself in His hands, He will bring you off more than conqueror through Him that has loved you."[7]

We cannot get into a detailed discussion of the investigative judgment here, but belief in that important doctrine can definitely help us live more effective lives in several ways.

a. The Vindication of God

Down through the centuries, Satan has falsely accused the Trinity and created doubt about Their love. In the investigative judgment the record finally will be set straight. The Bible tells us that after a complete review of the plan of salvation by unfallen beings, the Godhead fully and gloriously will be vindicated. It will be clearly established for all time that They can be trusted. Such an assurance can help establish our confidence in God today.

The apostle wrote, "God forbid: yea, let God be true, but every man a liar; as it is written, That thou mightest be justified in thy sayings, and mightest overcome when thou art judged" (Romans 3:4, KJV).

b. Our Value

The investigative judgment lets us know that God and the rest of the universe value each of us very highly. They spend large amounts of time learning about every person whose name is presented. It is an affirmation of the dignity of each one.

c. Atonement

In Old Testament times, the annual cleansing of the sanctuary took place on the Day of *Atonement.* That term can be defined as "at-one-ment," which applies to the cleansing of the sanctuary in heaven because that cleansing is a vital part of God's overall plan to bring us into oneness with Himself.

How that crucial oneness can be achieved is illustrated by the two times Jesus rid the earthly sanctuary of disreputable commerce. The area of the temple where the money-changers and dove-sellers had set up shop was the Court of the Gentiles. This was the outer ring of the temple complex and the only place the Gentiles were allowed to worship the God of Israel.

The selling and bartering going on there was like the clamor on the floor of the New York Stock Exchange. What got Christ so upset was that the activity and noise were making it impossible for the Gentiles to learn about Him. The bedlam was a barrier between Himself and the Gentile worshipers. So, He picked up a whip and tossed the merchants out on their collective ear.

The Savior did for the Gentiles what they could not do for themselves. And Christ can do the same for us today as He cleanses our hearts spiritually. The Savior loves us so much that He will take the initiative to get rid of anything that is a barrier between us and Him. There are barriers of discouragement, hurt, anger, anxiety, failure, and others. You may feel as helpless as the Gentiles, but Jesus is an expert at breaking down those barriers.

The Investigative Judgment tells us that if we choose to cooperate, Christ will send the Holy Spirit not only to change us from within but also to marshal whatever resources are necessary and arrange whatever life experiences are needed to draw us into close relationship, into at-one-ment, with Him.

d. Accountability

The investigative judgment reveals that accountability is very important to the Trinity. It is a fundamental value within the Godhead. They are modeling accountability for Themselves in Their willingness to let others review Their decision making. Even though the redeemed have nothing to fear in the judgment, it is a time of accountability for them, as well.

As we seek to reflect the values of the Trinity, we can build accountability into our lives today. Without accountability, we are liable to stray, to take the path of least resistance, and lose our direction. It is the only viable way for self-indulgent sinners to grow.

I have worked in the treasury department for more than two decades now. I deal with debits and credits, balance sheets and income statements, every day. Our staff makes hundreds of detailed and varied accounting entries every month. Everyone is fully aware that once a year "the auditors cometh." A team of professionals with CPA certification spends weeks reviewing our work—probing, asking questions, looking up documents, doing sample testing. Then they report our work to the entire conference constituency.

I had never experienced anywhere near that level of scrutiny before entering treasury work. Until then I had mostly scrutinized myself. That was certainly a much less stressful arrangement, but it had its weaknesses. It was pretty much like making an overeater accountable to the ice-cream man. I frequently gave myself a pass. If I messed up, I could variously blame other people, the weather, the food, the dog, the President of the United States, or whatever got me off the hook.

I will never forget the first time I went through an audit. I had been in treasury for two months. Perhaps it was just nerves, but whenever an auditor asked me a question, I'd blurt out an answer without pausing to think much about it. For some reason I got it into my head that they'd value a snappy answer more than a correct one. It took a month for my digestive tract to recover.

After experiencing many audits, I can sincerely say that I am glad we have them. I no longer get nervous and welcome the opportunity to grow and learn ways to do my work better.

The challenge is to introduce more accountability into my personal life. My wife is very good at letting me know when I have bad breath or when I've got my priorities mixed up. She also is one of my best editors. Feedback from others outside my family is very helpful, as well.

e. Hope for the Future

Because the cleansing of the sanctuary in heaven deals with the final eradication of sin, it becomes a source of tremendous hope. We can know for sure that evil is not eternal. There will be a day when suffering and wrong will end and be replaced by the shouts of joy from God's ecstatic redeemed.[8]

This chapter has explored some potential life applications of a few doctrines. It is now important for you to discover your own applications for all of our doctrines. Those discoveries hopefully will enable you to find increased healing and wholeness so that the words of Jesus can become a reality, "I am come that they might have life, and that they might have it more abundantly" (John 10:10, KJV).

---

1 http://www.amazon.com/How-Absolutely-Everything-Need-Know/dp/B000H2N1FC/sr=1-1/qid=1160308991/ref=sr_1_1/102-9076581-2223329?ie=UTF8&s=books, Dec. 26, 2006.

2 http://en.wikipedia.org/wiki/1000, Dec. 26, 2006.

3 http://www.articlesfactory.com/articles/health/life-and-health-in-the-year-1000.html, Dec. 26, 2006.

4 http://geography.about.com/library/weekly/aa011201c.htm, Dec. 26, 2006.

5 http://www.msnbc.msn.com/id/12923604/, Dec. 26, 2006.

6 Told in Stephen R. Covey, *The Seven Habits of Highly Effective People* (New York: Simon and Schuster, 1989), pp. 53, 54.

7 Ellen G. White, *Steps to Christ*, p. 72.

8 Ángel Manuel Rodríguez, "The Sanctuary and Its Cleansing," at http://www.adventistbiblicalresearch.org/documents/sanct&itscleansing.htm, Dec. 26, 2006.

Chapter 12

The Power of Love

Life in Israel was going along pretty much as normal. Then the nation was invaded by the Divine in a little backwater town called Bethlehem, and startling things began to happen. Shepherds were sipping Postum around a campfire, when suddenly the heavens lit up and flying choirs belted out heart-pounding hallelujahs. Supposedly heathen wise men felt compelled to withdraw hundreds of thousands of dollars from "Babylon Bank and Trust" and personally deposit it into the account of a peasant family hundreds of miles away. King Herod went completely off his rocker.

Twelve years later the best religious minds in Israel gathered for their annual Passover seminar to discuss the latest religious theories and conjectures, when a Teenager from Nazareth showed up, asked a few questions, and sent the whole pompous brain trust into a decades-long tailspin.

Eighteen years after that, a Carpenter from a nondescript village started loving and uplifting people in unheard-of ways. Hospitals were emptied, enemies became family, quarantined outcasts received major makeovers, the disenfranchised were highly honored, stinky dead people walked down Main Street, and common people poured into standing-room-only mass meetings.

It was impossible for God's infinite unselfishness to come in contact with a self-seeking society without fireworks.

The twelve disciples spent a lot of time pinching themselves to see if what they were witnessing each day with Jesus was real. One night in the familiar upper room, their world got turned upside down as never before. The Master, the One they had come to believe was the holy Messiah and Son of God, grabbed a basin of water and a towel, knelt down before them, and began scrubbing their dust-caked, camel-dung-spotted feet. Christ's dinner guests were incredulous. The whole thing was too much for Peter, and he quickly tucked his feet up and pulled away in horror.

Afterward Jesus said to them, "A new commandment I give unto you, That ye love one another; as I have loved you" (John 13:34, KJV). The commandment to love was not new. What was new was the extraordinary way the Savior chose to express it.

Then, just when the disciples could not imagine Christ's love for them going any deeper, they looked up on a hill just outside Jerusalem on Friday morning and saw Him hanging on a cross.

Jesus lived out the one-of-a-kind love that exists in the Godhead. What made His love so startling, so counterculture? It was consistently and intensely "other-oriented."

A friend of my wife's and mine came to visit. We hadn't seen him for many years. When he arrived in town, he phoned and told us to join him at a certain restaurant for supper. We met, found an empty booth, and ordered.

I started the conversation by asking about his family. He brought us up to speed one by one—wife, kids, grandkids. When he finished, I paused and waited a moment for him to ask something like, "So, enough about me. How are you and Ann doing, and your daughter Stefanie?" But there was silence.

To avoid any awkwardness, I went ahead and asked about his job. His answer came with considerable detail about appointments, tasks, meetings, frustrations, upcoming events, promotions. When he wound down, I paused again, a little longer this time, thinking perhaps he might inquire, "And how are *your* jobs coming? What's happening at work for you guys, huh?" Dead silence.

After what seemed like fifty years, I asked about his golf game. That produced a perky response with anecdotes and scores and a mini lesson on how to grip a putter properly. He ended and just sat there staring at the wall.

My mind raced for some other aspect of his fascinating life to inquire about. Thankfully my wife took over and posed a question of her own. Drinks came. We questioned him about his pets. The meal came. We questioned him about his ancestors. Dessert came. By this time our question reservoir was dry. So, we just sat there in a kind of conversation void eating cake and pie.

On the way home my wife and I looked at each other and laughed. We have this little running joke about how people love to talk about themselves and how rare it is for them to ask anything about us. The other day someone inquired, "So, how do you like Florida?" I was so surprised I told my wife about it later. Human beings tend to be self-absorbed. That's what sin does to us.

Jesus pointed His followers in the opposite direction. During His earthly ministry the Savior made it clear that He was setting up a counterculture kingdom. It was being established right before people's eyes. He said, " 'Repent, for the kingdom of heaven *is at hand*' " (Matthew 4:17, NKJV; italics supplied). Another translation puts it well, " 'Change your life. God's kingdom *is here*' " (*The Message*; italics supplied). When Jesus sent out the Twelve to preach, He told them to say, " ' "The kingdom of heaven *is at hand*" ' " (Matthew 10:7, NKJV; italics supplied). And in Matthew 12:28 we read, " '… surely the kingdom of God *has come upon you*' " (NKJV; italics supplied).

This kingdom would not contain armies, governments, territory, or buildings. It would not be so much a *realm* as a *reign*. Christ would rule in people's hearts.[1] The hallmark of life in the kingdom would be "other-oriented" love.

In the Sermon on the Mount, the Savior gave an overview of the startling values and relationships that would be present in the new kingdom. He taught that its citizens would behave in unusual ways, such as turning the other cheek, giving away the clothes off their back, walking twice as far as an antagonist compelled them to, and overcoming their enemies with love (see Matthew 5:38–44). In two key verses, the Lord summarized His thoughts:

" 'Live generously and graciously toward others, the way God lives toward you' " (Matthew. 5:48, *The Message*).

" 'Ask yourself what you want people to do for you, then grab the initiative and do it for *them.* Add up God's Law and Prophets and this is what you get' " (Matthew 7:12, *The Message;* italics in original).

After Jesus ascended to heaven, the church was supposed to become the visible, tangible embodiment of His new kingdom. "It is therefore the church's duty to display in an evil age of self-seeking, pride, and animosity the life and fellowship of the Kingdom of God."[2]

Divine love is so opposite from society's values and priorities, so counterintuitive, that it is inevitable that it will appear unusual. A good word to describe it might be "extravagant." That is what gives it power. The love revealed in and through the church often has a limited impact because it's not extravagant enough.

The Greeks had a certain word they used for common, everyday, human love—*eros.* "At its core, *eros* described that kind of love I give to what satisfies my desires, wins my admiration, or fulfills my appetites. *Eros* is love on a treasure hunt."[3] I scratch your back, and you scratch mine. When I don't get my way, I lash out. When you don't treat me as I think I deserve, I get angry. I can use you, manipulate you, and threaten you to get what I want. When you no longer meet my needs, I may even dump you.

The New Testament writers rejected that word and instead chose one that hadn't been used much by the Greeks, one in which they could inject their own unique meaning—*agape.* The ultimate example of agape love is the familiar verse, "For God so loved the world, that He gave His only begotten Son" (John 3:16 NKJV). The Trinity related to us on the basis of *our* need, not Theirs. While we were spitting in God's face, His beloved Son died in agony for each of us. We got the opposite of what we deserved. We got the Best when we deserved the least.

Victor Hugo's book *Les Misérables* captures well the theme of kingdom living. In the hard times of early nineteenth century France, a normally law-abiding citizen named Jean Valjean goes on a desperate search to find food for his widowed sister and her large family. While stealing a single loaf of bread, he's arrested and sentenced to five years in prison. His repeated attempts to escape lengthen the sentence to nineteen horrible years of work in the quarries among society's most degraded men. When he's finally released, Valjean is penniless and filled with hatred and resentment. The continuous rejection he receives after his release only hastens his further descent into corruption and distrust.

One day a kindly bishop sees his plight and offers Valjean a place to stay. At some point, however, overcome with temptation, the former prisoner steals some of the bishop's cherished silverware and dashes into the night. Captured, he's brought back to the bishop's home to confirm his thievery.

Fully expecting to hear words that would send him back to prison until he died, Valjean is stunned instead to hear the wise bishop tell the constable, "You are mistaken. This silver was my gift. But only part." He then walks into the dining room for a moment, returns, and continues, "You forgot the most valuable part." Gesturing to Valjean, he says, "You forgot to take the silver candlesticks."

One moment Valjean faces further imprisonment, and then he's suddenly given the gift of freedom and abundance by the very man he has so callously mistreated.

Before the overwhelmed, sobbing Valjean leaves, the bishop says to him, "You must never forget this moment. Your soul and your life have been bought back. You are not your own. From now on you belong to God." That marvelous encounter with God's extravagant love eventually changes Valjean forever.[4]

In order to manifest the values of Christ's kingdom, we don't need to do something as dramatic as the bishop did. God presents us with many opportunities if we are open to them. We don't need to be super-Christians, just willing ones with a divine perspective.

A speaker at a spiritual retreat told the story of a businessman who was eating at an out-of-town restaurant for lunch. When the waitress finally came, she seemed quite sullen and distracted. He had to repeat his order three times before she copied it down correctly. When the food came, she brought the wrong vegetable and drink. The final irritant came when she charged him twice for a single slice of apple pie.

When it was time to write in the tip, he stopped and pondered for a moment and then decided to leave a *40-percent tip* instead of the normal twenty. That evening he told his wife, who was the family bookkeeper, about the incident. He said, "At first I thought of lessening the waitress's tip dramatically because of the bad service. But then it struck me that she may be discouraged or hurting because of some issue in her life. With that in mind, I figured she needed an uplift rather than a scolding."

That's extravagant love. The businessman saw the waitress through God-enlightened eyes. He put her need ahead of his own and did something totally unexpected, the direct opposite of society's norm, because he chose grace.

Someone may react and say, "But she didn't *deserve* that tip!" That's the whole point. It is the "undeservedness" of kingdom love that marks it as divine.

Sometimes churches define success by baptisms, tithe, attendance, or programming. These things will be present in a mature church, but they are, at best, only secondary measures. When the apostle Paul wrote to churches, the thing he consistently looked for as the ultimate measure of success was the presence of faith, hope, and love, with the greatest of those being love. He said, "We give thanks to God always for you all, making mention of you in our prayers, remembering without ceasing your work of *faith,* labor of *love*, and patience of *hope* in our Lord Jesus Christ" (1 Thessalonians. 1:2, 3, NKJV; italics supplied). "We give thanks to the God and Father of our Lord Jesus Christ, praying always for you, since we heard of your *faith* in Christ Jesus and of your *love* for all the saints; because of the *hope* which is laid up for you in heaven" (Colossians. 1:3–5, NKJV; italics supplied).

Love will be the leading characteristic of the end-time church that "keep[s] the commandments of God," which Jesus said was summed up in loving God and our fellow humans (Revelation 14:12, NKJV; see Matthew 22:38–40).

Because love is so central, God has always been deeply concerned that it might become infected with society's values and lose its potency. The Lord made it clear to the people of Israel, " ' "You must not do as they do in Egypt, where you used to live, and you must not do as they do in the land of Canaan, where I am bringing you. Do not follow their practices" ' " (Leviticus 18:3, NIV).

"But God's people would not listen to his voice, and the specific reason given why his judgment fell first upon Israel and then nearly 150 years later upon Judah was the same: 'The people of Israel . . . had ... walked in the customs of the nations.' "[5]

If we allow our concept of love to become diluted by society's norms, it can easily slip down the list of priorities. If we fail to understand its unparalleled power, it can be replaced with lesser concerns.

One year when I was a young pastor, the largest church in my multichurch district was gearing up for evangelistic meetings that were about six months away. I recently had read the famous Spirit of Prophecy quote, "If we would humble ourselves before God, and be kind and courteous and tenderhearted and pitiful, there would be *one hundred conversions to the truth where now there is only one.*"[6] It seemed clear that the most powerful thing we could do to make the meetings a success was to help our church members become more loving and kind. We normally would expect about twenty-five baptisms. Imagine one hundred times that! Fantastic!

The book *Living God's Love* by Douglas Cooper had just come out at the Adventist Book Center and seemed like the perfect resource. I brought the idea to the church board and suggested that we use the book as our Sabbath School study guide for the next quarter, with one class still using the standard General Conference quarterly for those who preferred it. We would make the material available to everyone, and they could pay through a freewill offering at the end. I would write discussion questions for each chapter. I recalled for the board the words of Scripture, "Beloved, let us love one another, for love is of God; and everyone who loves is born of God and knows God. He who does not love does not know God, for God is love" (1 John 4:7, 8, NKJV). The vote in favor was unanimous.

On the very first Sabbath, I could tell by the tenor of the class discussions that the concepts in the book were already making an impact. The interactions were much more relational and personal in nature. The focus had suddenly moved from the head to the heart. The feedback was very positive.

After the eighth week, I received a phone call from the conference office saying that the president wanted to see me. I felt privileged because such a personal visit was somewhat of a rarity. We had been attempting some innovative ministries in the district, and I assumed that would be the topic of discussion.

When I arrived, the president came to the lobby and graciously ushered me into his office. He was about three inches taller than I am, with graying hair around the temples and a congenial, fatherly manner. After some small talk about our families, he said, "Now, Kim, I have heard that you are not using the regular Sabbath School quarterly in your congregation. Is that correct?"

I explained what we were doing and why.

He then leaned forward slightly and responded, "Well, you know that the General Conference sees the big picture, and they have mapped out their curriculum to make sure our people get a balanced spiritual diet. One quarter is the entrée, another is the potatoes, another is the vegetables. If you interrupt that cycle, our members will not be getting what they need." He strongly urged that we "get back on track."

I'm sure he meant well, but I was stunned. From my limited vantage point it seemed as though we had forgotten the ultimate purpose of all the Sabbath School quarterlies, that we had somehow gotten our "ends" and "means" mixed up, and lost sight of the centrality of love.

The Spirit of Prophecy tells us, "There is nothing that the Saviour desires so much as agents who will represent to the world His Spirit and His character. There is nothing that the world needs so much as the manifestation through humanity of the Saviour's love. All heaven is waiting for men and women through whom God can reveal the power of Christianity."[7]

Extravagant, counterculture love cannot flow from an empty vessel. Even though the ultimate goal is to help others, our own cup must first be filled before it can overflow to those around us. Everything begins by understanding how much we ourselves are loved.

> "I grew up knowing I was different, and I hated it. I was born with a cleft palate, and when I started school, my classmates made it clear to me how I looked to others: a little girl with a misshapen lip, crooked nose, lopsided teeth, and garbled speech.
>
> "When schoolmates asked, 'What happened to your lip?' I'd tell them I'd fallen and cut it on a piece of glass. Somehow it seemed more acceptable to have suffered an accident than to have been born different. I was convinced that no one outside my family could love me.
>
> "There was, however, a teacher in the second grade whom we all adored—Mrs. Leonard by name. She was short, round, happy—a sparkling lady.
>
> "Annually we had a hearing test . . . Mrs. Leonard gave the test to everyone in the class, and finally it was my turn. I knew from past years that as we stood against the door and covered one ear, the teacher sitting at her desk would whisper something, and we would have to repeat it back—things like 'The sky is blue' or 'Do you have new shoes?' I waited there for those words that God must have put into her mouth, those seven words that changed my life. Mrs. Leonard said in her whisper, 'I wish you were my little girl.' "[8]

Each of us needs to hear the words, "I wish you were My son, My daughter," spoken to us personally by God. Henri Nouwen reminds us that self-rejection is the great enemy of our spiritual life because it contradicts the voice that calls us Beloved. "Being the Beloved expresses the core truth of our existence."[9]

Jesus commanded us not only to love others but also to love ourselves: " ' "You shall love your neighbor *as yourself*" ' " (Matthew 19:19, NKJV; italics supplied). "Self-love and . . . inner security are essential to loving others. If a person is insecure about himself, dislikes himself, or even hates himself, he cannot love others. . . .

"... 'Self-love is having a feeling of dignity, a feeling of belonging, a feeling of worth-whileness, a feeling of adequacy—yet a healthy sense of humility.' "[10] Loving ourselves as God loves us leads to the opposite of selfishness; it frees us finally to be able to look beyond our own inner hurts, insecurities, and fears.

Deep love for others is not the product of willpower or guilt, it is a supernatural gift, given to us freely by the Holy Spirit. Only He can create within us a new heart of genuine caring. That love then needs to be nurtured, encouraged, and sustained by the loving community of fellow believers. When the love of one flags and grows weary from the pressures and trials of life, the other members of the body of Christ can come close and renew that person's energy and optimism through their own sympathy and support.

Extravagant love is not an obligation but an adventure. It should not be forced but rather unfold as serendipity. Each of us can reveal Christ's love through our own personality and temperament. It may be manifested in a small way or be supersized, behind the scenes or more obvious. Let extravagant love begin with your spouse and children then go with you as you move throughout the day at work, the church, or in the community.

Opportunities may present themselves at any time if we are available to the Holy Spirit. One of my religion professors in college told me that he had been trying for some time to find students who were hurting, so he could minister to them. Weeks went by without any obvious candidates. Then, out of frustration, he decided to put the responsibility back on God. He prayed, "Lord, You know who I need to connect with. You know where my steps will take me this day. If there is someone I can help, someone to whom I can manifest your caring and love, please make our paths cross and make me aware of who they are." He said that from that day forward more opportunities came his way than he could have imagined.

Often, the best opportunities to share God's extravagant love are tucked away in situations that tend to make us frustrated or upset. Those are ideal times to do the opposite of what would normally be expected.

It is, in fact, through loving others that we keep our own souls alive.

Viktor Frankl, an Austrian doctor, was imprisoned in one of Hitler's concentration camps. The prisoners were subjected to horrifying privation and oppression. They lacked adequate clothing, housing, and food, and were compelled to live in filth with no medical care. The sadistic guards treated them like animals.

Frankl, as a physician, carefully observed the health of the other prisoners and made an amazing discovery. "The people who kept their strength and sanity the longest were not the ones who by brute force or clever tricks obtained extra food, but rather those who tried to be helpful to the other prisoners and shared with them what little they had." [11]

The prophet Isaiah tells us,

"Is this not the fast that I have chosen:
To loose the bonds of wickedness,
To undo the heavy burdens,
To let the oppressed go free,
And that you break every yoke?
Is it not to share your bread with the hungry,
And that you bring to your house the poor who are cast out;
When you see the naked, that you cover him …?"
(Isaiah 58:6, 7, NKJV).

And then he tells us the effect that demonstrating such Christlike love will have on our own spiritual well-being: " 'Then your light shall break forth like the morning, / Your healing shall spring forth speedily' " (verse 8, NKJV).

In the parable of the sheep and the goats in Matthew 24:31–46, Jesus pictures for us what He expects His church to be doing in the world in the last days. He talks about the "sheep people" who have made love the central theme of their lives. These love dispensers feed those who are hungry—hungry not just for potatoes and carrots but for kindness and caring. They clothe those who feel naked—physically, emotionally, and spiritually. They quench people's thirst for acceptance and a listening ear. The Holy Spirit fills these sheep people with an intense desire to minister to family, church members, coworkers, and neighbors. He instills in them a special burden for those who have fallen badly or reached the end of their rope.

On the other hand, Jesus' parable also talks about "goat people." The main feature of goat love is that it is selective. These people say they would have been more than willing to help if they had only known it was Christ they were ministering to. Jesus' point is that it shouldn't matter at all who is in need. Nothing else should matter except that someone is hurting.

Pastor Jerry Cook tells the story of another pastor in his town who became involved in adultery. As a result, the man's marriage fell apart, and his ministry was destroyed. A year and a half later, this former pastor called Jerry Cook at 7:30 A.M. He asked if it would be all right if he and his new wife came to the worship service that morning.

"Of course," Jerry answered.

The pastor asked again if Jerry was sure it would be OK and received the same reply.

He then continued, "We've been trying for eight months now to find a place to worship. The last time we tried was a month ago. That morning we were asked from the pulpit to leave. . . . Frankly, I don't think we could handle it again if we were to come and be an embarrassment to you and be asked to leave. I just don't know what would happen; my wife is close to a nervous breakdown."

He began sobbing and then offered to sit in the video room where no one could see them.

Jerry answered, "Listen, you be there, and I'll welcome you at the door."

In the weeks and months that followed, the pastor met with Jerry and the church elders regularly and "wept his way back to God."

During this time a leading church official called and complained that the church had now opened the door to every broken-down pastor there is.

Jerry responded, "Praise the Lord! If they can't come here, where *can* they go? Someone has to be the end of the line for messed-up humanity."

He writes, "Today the church of Jesus Christ needs to make a bold commitment to love people. . . . Our whole life-style should tell people, 'If you come around here, we're going to love you. No matter who you are or what you've done or how you look, smell or behave, we're going to love you.' "[12]

It is relatively easy to teach biblical facts. It can be done by anyone with PowerPoint and a projector. It is far more difficult to love as Jesus loved. After I had preached for several Sabbaths on the importance of love, I remember a church member coming up to me and saying, "Pastor, why don't you give us some *real* spiritual meat? Why don't you preach on the end times and the mark of the beast?"

Those are important topics and ought to be fully explored. But we should never make the mistake of thinking that love is a "light" topic. Love is the heart of the gospel. It is the one word that Scripture uses to sum up the infinitely complex character of God. Love is not one of God's attributes among others; it is foundational, central, at the root of all else. *Love is the very essence of the Trinity life the church was created to reveal.*

"Can there be any power so great as the power of love?"[13] There is nothing more captivating and life-altering, nothing more healing and unifying, nothing more calculated to prepare people for the end time, than the love of God revealed collectively in and through His church. It is the mightiest, most effective outreach method by far.

The following Spirit of Prophecy quote looks forward to a time that the Trinity has longed to see for centuries, a time that can become a reality in our own day if we turn from lesser goals and give Their vision for the church the highest possible priority: "The members of the church, those whom He has called out of darkness into His marvelous light, are to show forth His glory. The church is the repository of the riches of the grace of Christ; and through the church will eventually be made manifest, even to 'the principalities and powers in heavenly places,' *the final and full display of the love of God.*" [14]

---

1 See George Eldon Ladd, *Jesus and the Kingdom* (Waco, Tex.: Word Books, 1964), p. 133.

2 George Eldon Ladd, *A Theology of the New Testament* (Grand Rapids, Mich.: Eerdmans, 1974), pp. 69, 115.

3 John Ortberg, *Love Beyond Reason,* p. 15.

4 Quoted from *Love Beyond Reason*, p. 136. Adaptation of the story from http://www.cliffsnotes.com/WileyCDA/LitNote/id-61.html, Dec. 28, 2006.

5 John R. W. Stott, *The Message of the Sermon On the Mount* (Downers Grove, Ill.: InterVarsity Press, 1978), p. 18.

6 Ellen G. White, *Testimonies for the Church*, 9:189; italics supplied.

7 Ellen G. White, *The Acts of the Apostles*, p. 600.

8 Quoted from *Love Beyond Reason*, pp. 148, 149.

9 Henri J. M. Nouwen, *Life of the Beloved* (New York: The Crossroad Publishing Company, 1999), p. 28.

10 Douglas Cooper, *Living God's Love* (Nampa, Idaho: Pacific Press®, 1975), p. 68.

11 John A. Howard, "Standing Tall," at http://www.profam.org/docs/jah/thc_jah_standtall.htm, Dec. 28, 2006.

12 Jerry Cook, *Love, Acceptance and Forgiveness* (Ventura, Calif.: Regal Books, 1979), pp. 9–12.

13 Ellen G. White, *The Retirement Years*, p. 76.

14 Ellen G. White, *The Acts of the Apostles*, p. 9; italics supplied.